ROUTLEDGE LIBRARY EDITIONS: GERMAN POLITICS

Volume 13

GERMANY TODAY

T0299987

GERMANY TODAY
Introductory Studies

Edited by
J. P. PAYNE

Routledge
Taylor & Francis Group

LONDON AND NEW YORK

First published in 1971

This edition first published in 2015
by Routledge
2 Park Square, Milton Park, Abingdon, Oxon, OX14 4RN

and by Routledge
711 Third Avenue, New York, NY 10017

Routledge is an imprint of the Taylor & Francis Group, an informa business

© 1971 Methuen & Co Ltd

British Library Cataloguing in Publication Data
A catalogue record for this book is available from the British Library

ISBN: 978-1-138-83837-6 (Set)
eISBN: 978-1-315-72630-4 (Set)
ISBN: 978-1-138-84788-0 (Volume 13)
eISBN: 978-1-315-72635-9 (Volume 13)
Pb ISBN: 978-1-138-84790-3 (Volume 13)

Publisher's Note
The publisher has gone to great lengths to ensure the quality of this reprint but points out that some imperfections in the original copies may be apparent.

Disclaimer
The publisher has made every effort to trace copyright holders and would welcome correspondence from those they have been unable to trace.

Germany Today

Introductory Studies

Edited by J. P. PAYNE

Methuen & Co Ltd
11 New Fetter Lane, London E.C.4

First published 1971 by Methuen & Co Ltd
11 New Fetter Lane, London E.C.4
© 1971 Methuen & Co Ltd
Printed in Great Britain by
Richard Clay (The Chaucer Press) Ltd
Bungay, Suffolk

SBN (hardbound) 416 20260 8
SBN (paperback) 416 20270 5

Distributed in the U.S.A.
by Barnes & Noble Inc.

Contents

Editor's Introduction

Anyone interested in the study of the German Federal Republic and the German Democratic Republic cannot complain about shortage of information. Quite apart from being able to go and see for himself what Germany is like he can choose from among the host of German newspapers and periodicals which are available abroad, he can read the work of Germans and foreigners on present-day Germany, he can avail himself of the facilities of German cultural centres throughout the world, he can listen to radio and television broadcasts either from Germany or about Germany.

No one would doubt that it is valuable to have so much information at one's disposal. Sheer quantity is however no guarantee of quality. Even if a student of Germany abroad regularly reads a German newspaper, has he thereby provided for himself an adequate source of information about the contemporary German scene? What reservations must he have in mind if, for example, this source is *Der Spiegel*? Does the editor have a particular axe to grind? Are his reports biased? If one is confronted with the statement that the West German 'economic miracle' came about through the German people's capacity for hard work – and this is quite likely in the course of one's reading – will one be able to measure this statement against the actual economic conditions that prevailed during the period of recovery? If one learns that the German social security system is one of the most advanced in the world, will one be able to make a mental reservation about the unbalanced distribution of wealth?

The problem is that questions such as these require some

familiarity with issues spanning several disciplines which may deter the student by the unfamiliarity of their method and the strangeness of their vocabulary. Although their views are of decisive influence in the development of advanced industrial societies, the economist and the sociologist, for example, tend to present their arguments in language which was not coined with the layman in mind. Yet without a minimum of familiarity with the problems that concern the economist, the sociologist and experts in other fields of knowledge, it is impossible for the individual to organize his work on Germany and form his own balanced critical opinion on contemporary issues. The present book, written by experts from different fields and with different interests, attempts to provide the basis for an understanding of issues which affect the daily life of Germans in the GFR and the GDR. The various authors have formulated their ideas with the general reader in mind; the individual articles range over a wider variety of problems and the method of presentation is less specialized than would be the case in articles written for scientific journals in the respective fields. However, the standards of accuracy and objectivity they seek to uphold are no less rigorous.

The subjects covered include some of the most important aspects of the development of modern Germany. Germany has become one of the clearest examples of the effects of the Cold War, the division of Germany reflecting the deadlock of the world powers. R. Cecil, a historian, examines this crucial and extraordinarily complex problem. Since the turn of the century Germany has had a rapid succession of different modes of government: monarchy, pluralistic democracy, fascism and yet another form of pluralistic democracy. R. B. Tilford, a political scientist, examines how West Germans have adjusted to the latest mode of government. Those who have been to Berlin have experienced at first hand the extent to which recent history has affected the lives of the average German. J. Fijalkowski, a sociology professor, who lives in Berlin, is admirably placed to examine the forces which shape the lives of the citizens of the GDR as well as those of the GFR. His contribution covers a

viii

wide range of issues from house-purchase to old-age pensions. M. E. Streit, who has worked on the professional staff of the Council of Economic Advisers to the German Government, has been involved at first hand with the running of an economy whose problems many a Western country would gladly exchange for its own. W. Meyer-Erlach and myself, both literary critics with a deep interest in contemporary Germany, examine, respectively, the present cultural and educational 'scene', and the press.

Though this book attempts to provide a basis for an in-the-round study of Germany today, it cannot be comprehensive. Many fields of great interest and importance have, regretfully, been left unexplored: the influence of religion, the functioning of the Provincial and Federal Parliaments, the role of the armed forces, the geography of Germany, the question of the Germans' relation to their past, to mention only a few. The GDR has, through shortage of space, received less attention than one would like. However, it is hoped that the individual contributions, each of which is followed by a bibliography of selected literature, will provide a stimulus to further study.

The Contributors

After taking a degree in history at Cambridge in 1935, R. Cecil worked for over thirty years in the British Foreign Service. During this time he was Consul-General in Hanover from 1955 to 1957 and Cultural Counsellor in Bonn from 1957 to 1959. In 1968 he was made Reader in Contemporary German History at the University of Reading where his teaching commitments include courses in the Graduate School of Contemporary European Studies.

After graduating (in German and French) from University College, London, R. B. Tilford spent four years as a journalist in Bonn, Berlin and Munich. Since 1964 he has been a Lecturer (subsequently Senior Lecturer) in German Regional Studies at the University of Surrey. In 1970 he received his M.Sc. (Econ.)

in Comparative Government from the London School of Economics. His publications include several papers on German politics in British political science journals and a book in conjunction with R. J. C. Preece, *Federal Germany: Political and Social Order* (London, Oswald Wolff, 1969).

J. Fijalkowski, born in 1928, studied philosophy, sociology and psychology in the Humboldt University in East Berlin and the Free University of West Berlin. From 1954 to 1963 he was an assistant lecturer (*Wissenschaftlicher Assistent mit Lehraufträgen*) at the Institute for Sociology and was in charge of some research projects in the Institute for Political Science at the Free University, where, in 1964, he was made *akademischer Rat*. In 1970 he received his professorship. His main areas of interest comprise comparative constitutional theory, social history and political sociology. His publications include a work on the political philosophy of Carl Schmitt and numerous contributions to scientific journals and encyclopedias in the fields of Sociology and Political Science.

M. E. Streit was an undergraduate student of economics at the University of Saarbrücken from 1959 to 1963 when he took the degree of *Diplom-Volkswirt*. From 1963 until 1966 he was a teaching assistant at the same university and undertook research. In 1966 he gained his doctorate and was appointed to the professional staff of the German Council of Economic Advisers (*Sachverständigenrat zur Begutachtung der gesamtwirtschaftlichen Entwicklung*). Dr Streit is at present Volkswagen Lecturer in Economics at the University of Reading and teaches at the Graduate School of Contemporary European Studies there. His main interests are economic policy, especially regional policy and business cycles policy. His publications include a regional study concerned with economic prospects for the Saar (written in collaboration with O. Sievert) and contributions to several periodicals concerned with economic affairs.

After an education disrupted by the war, with periods of study at Jena and Berlin, W. Meyer-Erlach held executive positions in industrial firms both in Germany and Canada. He took up his university studies again in Canada at the University of Toronto in 1959, gaining his B.A. in 1964. He has been involved in the development of German studies at the satellite colleges of the University of Toronto, Scarborough and Erindale, since 1966. After taking his comprehensive examination in 1968, he is now working on his Ph.D. dissertation on literature and society in the mid-nineteenth century. He holds the position of Assistant Professor in German at Erindale College, University of Toronto.

I myself graduated from Cambridge in 1964 with a degree in Modern Languages (German and French) and after post-graduate studies in German Literature at Cambridge moved, in 1967, to Reading University as an Assistant Lecturer in the German Department. While at Reading, I taught a course on contemporary German politics and institutions in the Graduate School of Contemporary European Studies. Since September 1969 I have been teaching at Erindale College, University of Toronto as an Assistant Professor in German.

I should like to thank W. A. Coupe and R. Cecil for their help in the early stages of the planning of this book, and also W. Meyer-Erlach, Mrs G. Sterling, Mrs M. McGarvey, Mrs K. Younger, Mrs Brigitte Krause, and my wife who have assisted me in the actual preparation.

J. P. Payne
Erindale College
University of Toronto

1 Germany and Reunification

R. CECIL

History is not just what happened; it is also – and perhaps more significantly – what people have come to believe happened. This can be illustrated by two episodes separated in time by ten years. The first took place in the spring of 1959 near the zonal border between the German Federal Republic (GFR) and the 'so-called' German Democratic Republic (GDR). I was looking across the barbed-wire and the ploughed strip at some cherry trees in flower, when a middle-aged German farmer came up to me and remarked that, until the wire went up, those trees had belonged to him. I was on the point of expressing my sympathy, when he added, 'That's what your Churchill, Roosevelt and Stalin did to me!' Instead of the words of sympathy, I felt obliged to ask whether Hitler had not also had something to do with it. This put an abrupt end to the conversation.

The second episode took place in Bad Godesberg during the federal election campaign of September 1969. Günter Grass was addressing a packed meeting, at which an unusually high proportion of young people was present. Whenever foreign policy was mentioned, an elderly man persisted in shouting, 'What about Koenigsberg?' (This famous East Prussian city has now been incorporated in the USSR.) Finally Grass turned to him. 'Koenigsberg', he said, 'was gambled away through German folly and you will have to get used to it.' This reply evoked no murmurs of discontent, but rather a round of applause.

Various interpretations could, of course, be placed on these stories. They could be taken to illustrate the generation gap, the growing political sophistication of the German people, or the simple fact that time is the great healer. But does this mean that the issue of reunification is gradually being forgotten and that Germans are becoming content to live divided? He would be a bold man who would defend this thesis, even though *Deutschlandpolitik* was not a major issue in the 1969 election campaign. Outside Germany, there is indeed a trend in the direction of 'letting sleeping dogs lie'. It is a comparatively recent development. In 1960 Anthony Nutting wrote in *International Affairs*,[1] 'No European security arrangement would be worth anything if Germany remained divided within it.' It is probable that at that date the great majority of experienced observers in Western capitals would have agreed with him. If this is no longer equally true today, we must investigate the reasons for this change of attitude and the impact it is having, or will have, upon the Germans themselves.

In spite of the H-bomb and the intensity of the Cold War, the generation that has grown up in Europe since 1945 has in two respects been more fortunate than that which grew up after 1918. No one seriously doubts, in Germany or elsewhere, that Hitler intended war. The young people of former belligerent countries have therefore been largely spared the tedious and inconclusive arguments about war guilt, which perplexed the older generation. Appeasement on one side then faced resentful nationalism on the other. Secondly, Hitler's persistence in fighting his war to the bitter end, obliging his opponents to occupy Germany, effectively prevented the emergence of a 'stab in the back' legend (*Dolchstoss-Legende*); the young generation in Germany has had to face reality from the start, instead of escaping into a world of illusion, in which the anti-rational ideology of Nazism could take root.

The reality of 1945 was harsh indeed, so much so that some years elapsed before Germans could allow themselves relaxation from the struggle for bare existence in order to reflect on territorial problems. In 1951, when the West German Institute of Public Opinion asked people what they thought was the most important question facing Germany, only 18 per cent replied reunification, compared with 45 per cent who replied that it was

2

the economic conditions.[2] The German people were adrift in the tides of the Cold War over which they had little control; it was still the era of *ohne mich* (or 'count me out'). The economic policies of Adenauer and Erhard, however, were rapidly curing the physical and material ills of the people and thus laying the foundation of twenty years of *CDU/CSU* predominance, which only came to an end in October 1969.

But if the West Germans were adrift, they were not altogether helpless; Adenauer's hand was on the tiller and he had had from the beginning a very clear idea in which direction he wanted to go. As early as October 1945 in a press interview he had expressed the view that, 'The Soviet occupied part is lost to Germany for an unforeseeable period . . .'[3] Accordingly he set himself the priority task of recovering the sovereignty of West Germany, which could only be achieved by full co-operation with the Western powers. The intensification of the Cold War, particularly the outbreak of the Korean War in the summer of 1950, gave him his opportunity and he was able to trade West German infantry against a growing measure of equality with the sovereign powers of the West. It was on this issue of German rearmament that the present Federal German President, Gustav Heinemann, left Adenauer's cabinet in the autumn of 1950.

Schumacher and the *SPD* did not agree with Adenauer's priorities. 'Any policy that tries to buy equality with military contributions is condemned to failure', asserted Schumacher.[4] But failure was relative, depending on the objective adopted. The West German people did not regard the 'economic miracle' and progress towards the economic integration of western Europe as failure. It was only when a substantial degree of success had been achieved in reaching these objectives that people began to ask themselves why nothing had happened about reunification. In 1957 the Institute that had posed the question of priorities in 1951 put the same query again. This time the result was almost exactly reversed: 43 per cent put reunification first, while 18 per cent still thought that improved economic conditions was the most important matter facing Germany.

Adenauer had his answer ready. 'There were those in Germany who thought that for us the choice was either a policy for Europe or a policy for German unity . . .' But Adenauer knew better; as he explained in his *Memoirs*, 'Only when the West was strong might there be a genuine point of departure for peace negotiations . . .'5 It was, in short, the policy of reunification through strength and Adenauer adhered to it unswervingly until his retirement in the autumn of 1963. He also had a second answer: built into the negotiations with the Western Allies, beginning with the abortive Bonn Conventions (1952) and concluding with the agreements by which the Federal Republic entered NATO in 1955, was a deal by which, in return for German troops and a German renunciation of force as a means of achieving reunification or a modification of frontiers, the Western powers committed themselves to re-garding reunification as 'a fundamental aim of their policy'. Adenauer thus shared out responsibility for the success or failure of his policy, as the West Germans will no doubt remind their Allies one of these days.

Did Adenauer himself believe in the policy of strength or was it a façade behind which he concentrated his attention on western Europe? It is a question to which we shall never know the answer. His *Memoirs*, detailed as they are, read like political tracts and reveal little about the real working of his mind. It must be said, however, that there were always those who were ready to renew his conviction that the fateful choice of priorities between European integration and reunification, which he had made at the beginning of his career as Chancellor, was the right one. In August 1955, distressed by the degree of *détente* achieved at the Geneva 'Summit' conference, he wrote to John Foster Dulles, who replied that he thought there was a good chance that reunification on Adenauer's terms could be brought about within a few years, if the West stood firm. After Dulles's death in 1959, the role of fortifying Adenauer in his faith in

4

standing firm was taken over by de Gaulle, until the final posture became one of almost complete rigidity.

Adenauer's conviction that he was right – the scarcely escapable delusion of a man who has held office continuously for fourteen years – was no longer shared either by the Anglo-Saxon countries or by a majority of the West Germans. On this issue, even his own party, the *CDU*, split between the Gaullists and the *Atlantiker*; Gerhard Schroeder, who became Foreign Minister after the 1961 elections, was numbered among the latter. However, another question was asked at that time, especially by the Gaullists, to which there will never be an answer, except in the unlikely event that the Kremlin opens its uncensored archives without restriction to Western historians. Did Khruschev ever have any real intention of settling the German problem?

Valuable testimony on this crucial point is to be found in the Memoirs of Hans Kroll, who was German Ambassador in Moscow from 1958 to 1962. This was a period when, in spite of the set-back of the abortive 'Summit' conference at Paris in 1960, Khruschev showed a continuous interest in negotiations with the West over Berlin and, in a lesser degree, the German problem as a whole. His main concern was to negotiate with the Americans, but he also displayed unmistakable interest in negotiating with Adenauer. Adenauer had visited Moscow in 1955 and Khruschev repeatedly intimated to Kroll that a return invitation was overdue. His conversations with the Ambassador, which took place in an atmosphere of mutual confidence and respect, were undertaken in the shadow of Soviet threats to sign a peace treaty with the GDR and thus withdraw unilaterally from the 1945 agreements on which the four-power occupation of Berlin was based. Khruschev did not, of course, reveal his intentions in the preliminaries, but on one occasion he did make it plain to Kroll that, rather than fulfil his threat to sign a peace treaty with the GDR alone, he would prefer to sign one with a confederation of the two Germanies. The exact status of Berlin within this confederation was never made clear; at one point

5

the city was referred to as the prospective capital of the confederation; but the possibility was evidently considered that West Berlin, as a separate entity, or free city, might become a third element in the confederation.

These modalities were not investigated; there was no direct Russo-German negotiation and no invitation to Khruschev, in spite of Kroll's pleas and the entirely permissive attitude in all Western capitals except Paris. Adenauer, drawing upon his long memory of German history, persisted in the belief, either real or feigned, that direct negotiation with Moscow would revive in Western minds suspicions of the Russo-German Rapallo Pact of 1922. A polite but evasive reply was sent to Moscow in February 1962 and in the following April the tortuous Russo-American negotiations were resumed. Their course, however, was not made any smoother by a disastrous leakage in Bonn, giving rise to strong suspicions that the Bonn government was neither prepared to negotiate, nor to allow its allies to do so. With de Gaulle as *tertius gaudens*, relations between Bonn and the Anglo-Saxons had reached a very low point. In Bonn criticisms were voiced that the Americans were seeking a deal with Moscow at German expense, while in Washington the impression was growing that Adenauer wanted Americans to die, if need be, in defence of Berlin, but not to seek a negotiated settlement of the dispute with the USSR. Ambassador Kroll was withdrawn from Moscow and Ambassador Grewe from Washington, and ruffled feathers gradually fell back into place.

Our question whether Khruschev meant business, or wished only to disrupt Western unity, remains. All that one can add in answer to it is that Adenauer himself seems to have believed that Khruschev was serious in seeking negotiations. In July 1963 he told de Gaulle that Khruschev's approach was probably to be explained in terms of his knowing that, once Adenauer had retired, he (Khruschev) would never be able to negotiate with Erhard, since (as Adenauer observed to de Gaulle) his designated successor, Erhard, 'would not feel himself strong enough to take responsibility for the result'.[6] This remark seems to pre-

6

suppose belief that serious negotiation was on the cards; otherwise there would have been no point in this gratuitous insult to Erhard.

However that may be, Erhard did eventually decide to issue the long deferred invitation to Khruschev to visit Bonn, but the latter's eclipse in October 1964 finally put a stop at the end of this chapter. As Kroll has it, 'The removal of the Soviet party and government chief did indeed mean the end of the provisional willingness of the Kremlin to try for a relaxation, in direct negotiations with the Federal Republic, of the relations between the two countries and thereafter a normalization and *rapprochement*.'[7]

Kroll drew a further conclusion which retains its validity to this day: 'The better the relations between Bonn and Moscow, the cooler they will be between Moscow and the GDR.'[8] Khruschev seems to have been willing to cold-shoulder Ulbricht in a way that his successors have hesitated to do. It is perhaps fortunate that the long delayed treaty between the USSR and the GDR was signed in June 1964 – a few months before Khruschev's disappearance from the scene. The treaty, valid for twenty years, cannot have given Ulbricht much joy; Article 9 affirms that Soviet rights based on international agreements, including the 1945 Potsdam agreement, are in no way diminished. Khruschev, in spite of earlier threats, had settled for a solution which fell far short of giving Ulbricht his sovereignty or establishing Berlin as the undisputed capital of his state.

It has been necessary to devote this much space to reviewing the negative aspect of Adenauer's foreign policy in order to apportion responsibility for the existing stalemate, a stalemate which may well cause greater distress to the German people in the future than it appears to do at the present. Our review has established that there was at least one period of recent history when two of Adenauer's major allies seemed more anxious than he was himself to achieve *détente* and negotiations with the USSR. Admittedly Washington and London were more interested in negotiating about the Berlin problem than about Germany as a whole; but this was understandable. Berlin was the immediate cause of tension and it was the belief of the Anglo-Saxon powers that a reduction of tension was the pre-requisite of meaningful negotiation over the whole field.

All that Adenauer was prepared to offer was what he described in the conversation with de Gaulle already mentioned (July 1963) as 'a ten-year truce (*Burgfriede*) in the German question'. This was a strange proposal, in that it assumed that time was working for West Germany, whereas the contrary was the case. The construction of the Berlin Wall in August 1961, however repugnant on humanitarian grounds, had in fact stabilized the situation. The GDR was no longer subject to a continuous loss of self-respect and of manpower. An economic recovery had begun and was stimulated by the economic reforms of 1963. The subsequent expansion of industrial production can justly be described as 'a mini-miracle'. Today the GDR has far surpassed Czechoslovakia as an industrial nation and, indeed, comes ninth in the world rating. This is not to say that there is no discontent. Housing and the supply of consumer goods lag behind; there are some signs of student dissatisfaction with the lack of intellectual freedom; but 17 June 1953 is no more than a memory. The GDR has consolidated its position.

The recognition of this unwelcome fact was one of the first changes introduced by the *CDU/SPD* coalition, which came to power in December 1966. In a speech in the following June the new Federal Chancellor, Kurt Georg Kiesinger, specifically said, 'Time is not on our side . . . that is why this government has decided in favour of a new, mobile policy with regard to the East, both with regard to our Eastern neighbours as well as in German domestic relations with those responsible in the other part of Germany.' There is already here a change of tone. Ulbricht may not relish being treated as part of a domestic problem, but at least he is no longer denigrated as representing 'the Zone' or the 'so-called' GDR. Later, when Kiesinger received a letter from Willi Stoph, Chairman of the Council of

8

Ministers in the GDR, he replied personally. This was a departure from the precedent set by Adenauer in January 1951, when he merely replied by means of a statement in the *Bundestag* to Otto Grotewohl's letter of November 1950, containing proposals for reunification. (Grotewohl was Stoph's predecessor.)

Before the formation of the Grand Coalition, however, West Berlin, under the guidance of its Mayor, Willy Brandt, had already shown the way ahead. Towards the end of 1963 the city administration, negotiating directly with the GDR authorities, had signed an agreement enabling West Berliners to visit relatives in East Berlin over Christmas 1963 and New Year 1964. This approach to the Berlin problem on humanitarian grounds was in strong contrast to legal objection that West Berlin, by negotiating with the GDR, had made a concession to Communist claims that the city was a political unit separate from the Federal Republic. Nothing illustrates the defeatism of the legalist attitude more clearly than the retaliation for the building of the Wall adopted by NATO, which included restrictions on the granting of temporary travel documents for East Germans wishing to visit the West. As it was tacitly agreed that trade should go on, the restrictions operated mainly in the area of education, science, culture and sport. In other words, those sections of the community which in Communist countries have shown themselves most susceptible to Western influence were the ones to suffer. Brandt, by acting from genuinely humanitarian motives, was able to avoid such self-defeating tactics. Even before becoming Foreign Minister and Vice-Chancellor in 1966 he had begun the attempt, without which reunification was, and is, a lost cause, to renew the human foundation on which German unity must ultimately rest, namely the feeling that the parts belong together.

By pre-empting this card, statesmen in the Federal Republic were able to expose the hollowness of the GDR propaganda and the fear of *rapprochement* that it concealed. Stoph's letter to Kiesinger of May 1967, which has already been mentioned, although couched in the form of a proposal for normalizing relations and relaxing tension, in fact stipulated certain concessions which the Federal Republic must make before negotiations could begin. These included abandonment of the claim to represent all Germany (*Alleinvertretung*), recognition of the GDR within its existing frontiers and a joint programme of disarmament, leading to the formation of a nuclear-free zone in central Europe. In short, the Federal Republic was required to discard its trumps before beginning to play the hand.

Kiesinger in his reply emphasized that he had not proposed a political confrontation. 'On the contrary, what is wanted is a discussion of how we can prevent Germans in this time of imposed separation from losing human contact with one another.' He therefore suggested dealing with the sixteen practical, non-controversial questions which he had announced in the *Bundestag* on 12 April 1967. These included improved facilities for travel and exchange of parcels, freer movement of student, youth and sports groups, as well as common policies on such matters as linked systems of electric power and construction of roads, bridges and telephone lines. In September, however, Stoph replied reiterating his previous demands and, after a barrage of hostile propaganda, he added to them in May 1968 by insisting that, if the Federal Republic wished to normalize relations, it must abandon the emergency legislation (*Notstandsgesetze*) which was at that time the subject of acrimonious debate.

Two main conclusions may be drawn from this abortive correspondence. First, the apparent willingness of the GDR to embark on discussions vanished as soon as the changed attitude of Bonn showed that these could actually take place; this despite the fact that Kiesinger's reply, even if he did not formally recognize the GDR, made a first concession to Stoph by admitting the existence of an authority in the other part of Germany with which binding agreements could be concluded. Secondly, the defensive attitude of the GDR, coupled with the unleashing of anti-Bonn propaganda, which would in any case have prejudiced the decision to negotiate on Stoph's terms, displayed acute anxiety and loss of confidence. This would seem attributable to developments in eastern Europe and primarily in Czechoslovakia. We must therefore turn to a consideration of the Federal Republic's *Ostpolitik* at that time.

As we have seen, Schroeder, who continued as Foreign Minister under Erhard, looked to Washington and was sympathetic to ideas of *détente* in Europe. As far back as 1962 he had said at a federal conference of the *CDU*: 'Our aim is a just European order, based upon peaceful agreements, in which all peoples can live freely together as good neighbours. The nations of the Warsaw Pact also belong to Europe.' The GDR might be a signatory of the Warsaw Pact, but she evidently was not a nation; the more willing Schroeder was to cultivate eastern Europe, the more isolated the GDR became. Playing his highest card, Schroeder opened trade missions in Poland, Hungary, Bulgaria and Romania and embarked on the negotiations which later led to full diplomatic relations with the last-mentioned country, even at the expense of the 'Hallstein' doctrine (whereby Bonn is reluctant to have relations with a country recognizing the legal existence of the GDR). It was the heyday of 'polycentrist' theories, predicated on the assumption that the USSR was too preoccupied with the challenge of China to reassert her authority among her European satellites.

The threat to Ulbricht was very real. As Professor R. V. Burks had pointed out: 'While intrabloc trade was tending to stagnate, West Germany's trade with eastern Europe was growing steadily, increasing in absolute value ten times between 1950 and 1967.'[9] Romania and Bulgaria were running deficits in their trade with the Federal Republic and offers of credit would clearly have political as well as economic implications. The intrusion of the Federal Republic would not only disturb the pattern of production and exchange of goods laid down within COMECON (Council for Mutual Economic Assistance – the trading bloc led by the USSR), but would detract from the key position held in it by the GDR. After the establishment of

diplomatic relations between Bonn and Bucharest in January
1967, Ulbricht set out to show that continuation of Schroeder's
Ostpolitik was incompatible with Brandt's new *Deutschlandpolitik.*

Ulbricht is a man of resource—indeed he is, with Tito,
the only European Communist leader to have held power
unbrokenly since the end of the war. He not only spoke harsh
words to Kiesinger, but he invoked the help of Moscow and
Warsaw to bring pressure to bear on the weaker brethren of the
Pact. Hungary and Bulgaria were restrained from following the
example of Romania, and Czechoslovakia (still led by the 'hard-
liner', Novotny) was held down to a level of representation with
Bonn no more important than consular functions and a trade
mission. An 'Ulbricht doctrine' was also devised to act as a
'Hallstein doctrine' in reverse, debarring members of the Warsaw
Pact from establishing diplomatic relations with Bonn until the
Federal Republic had given formal recognition to the GDR.
Leonid Brezhnev, visiting East Berlin in the spring of 1967
remarked, much to Ulbricht's satisfaction, that hidden in the
Federal Republic's outstretched hand was a great stone.

Ulbricht's reactions can hardly have come as a surprise to
Brandt, but the latter said in a book published in Germany in
1968 that he 'did not expect the government of the Soviet
Union to identify itself, to the extent to which this has happened,
with the hostile attitude of East Berlin towards the government
of the Grand Coalition.'[10] It would have been unrealistic to
expect Brandt to abandon his promising line of approach to
eastern Europe; indeed he brought to a successful conclusion
Schroeder's negotiations with Romania and in 1968 also resumed diplomatic relations with Yugoslavia, which had been
broken off in 1957 in deference to the 'Hallstein doctrine'. But
he made public the fact that, in pursuing this policy of *détente*
and normalization, he was not seeking to stir up trouble within
the Soviet bloc. 'It is not our goal', he wrote in an article
published in April 1968, 'nor even a peripheral intention of our
new Eastern policy to isolate the GDR, nor do we intend to

create or exploit differences between the Soviet Union and her allies – often as this is claimed in Eastern propaganda.'[11]

When these words were written, however, the train of events in Czechoslovakia, fired by Novotny's removal in January 1968, had created a situation which must have seemed to Brezhnev and Ulbricht to give the lie to Brandt and justify the forebodings of their propaganda. According to the propaganda line adopted later in the summer, the Czech people, betrayed by their leaders, were again in danger of becoming victims of German pressure, even if exerted in a less brutal and barefaced manner than had been the case in 1938. The rational counter-argument of the Czechs that, in order to re-equip their basic industries to serve the common cause they needed German machinery and credits, fell on deaf ears. German capital was no more permissible in 1968 than American capital had been in 1947, when Stalin ruled in the Kremlin. In June, Dubcek abolished censorship in Czechoslovakia and Ulbricht, uneasily mindful that 'the truth shall make ye free', found himself obliged to jam German language broadcasts from Prague and prohibit importation of newspapers circulating among the German-speaking communities still living in parts of Bohemia.

As Brezhnev still hesitated to act, Ulbricht seems to have decided to force his hand by showing that two could play Dubcek's game. As Professor Burks puts it, 'Ulbricht summoned the *Volkskammer* into extraordinary session on 9 August and proposed trade negotiations with Bonn at ministerial level, suddenly dropping the precondition of West German diplomatic recognition, to which he had hitherto adamantly held.'[12] Whatever effect this move may have had in Moscow, the Russians finally went into action on 21 August with their obedient allies. German troops did indeed enter Czechoslovakia again, but this time the troops belonged to the GDR's People's Army. Brezhnev not only slammed the door, he also put on it a notice to the effect that no member of the 'Socialist bloc' would in future be permitted to act in a way that, in the opinion of the others, would endanger the solidarity of all. No alternative 'roads to Socialism' on the Yugoslav model would be allowed. The Warsaw Pact is a shot-gun marriage and incompatibility provides no ground for divorce. It is clear that, while Ulbricht welcomed this tightening of bonds in 1968, a day may come when the 'Brezhnev doctrine' will be applied against the GDR, if the enticements of the Federal Republic become irresistible.

Since combined action by Warsaw powers has closed the back-door to normalization, which Bonn's *Ostpolitik* seemed at one moment to have partly prised open, only one road remains – the road to Moscow, which Kroll vainly recommended earlier. Brandt, in his speeches and writings made quite clear that he knew this relationship to be the crucial one, even before Brezhnev announced that the fence round the 'Socialist bloc' was charged with electricity. In the article from which I have already quoted, Brandt wrote: 'Of central importance is our relationship to the leading power in the group of socialist states, the Soviet Union. This is self-evident from an assessment of the facts of world affairs, the power relationships and the pattern of interests in eastern Europe.'[13] We must therefore now attempt to look at the problem through the windows of the Kremlin.

The value of the GDR to the bloc in general and to the USSR in particular scarcely needs to be emphasized. A glance at the map shows that, so long as Soviet troops remain in the GDR, they have a stranglehold on Poland and, as events have so recently demonstrated, a point of entry into Czechoslovakia. Quite apart from the asset represented by the GDR's *Volks-armee*, these strategic advantages are not ones that the USSR would lightly abandon. Even if the Kremlin is now inclined to regard NATO as 'a paper tiger', the need to maintain the solidarity of the bloc has never been more acute. Its disintegration would involve for the USSR not only great material disadvantages, but a loss of prestige and ideological reputation such that she could scarcely continue to claim leadership of the Communist world. A 'palace revolution' in Moscow would be a likely consequence.

14

In the economic sphere the GDR is scarcely less important; as a supplier of capital equipment her importance has increased as that of Czechoslovakia has declined. Professor Karl Kaiser has stressed the GDR's relationship to COMECON in these words: 'Among all members of this grouping, the COMECON share in her foreign trade is the highest, the Western share (excluding the Federal Republic's) the lowest. She is therefore an indispensable partner.'[14] Industrial production in the GDR continues to rise, both in volume and quality, and it is estimated that production *per capita*, in spite of the large proportion of women in the labour force, far exceeds that in the Soviet Union. It might, of course, be argued that, if some form of German confederation comes about on terms safeguarding 'the achievements of Socialism' in the GDR and loosening the Federal Republic's ties with the West, the bloc, instead of losing a daughter, will gain a son-in-law. The economic arguments in favour of closer association between eastern Europe and Germany as a whole are, indeed, indisputable. Marxism-Leninism, however, as an ideology, has long ceased to be one in which economic considerations play a dominant role. The very fact that standards of living might rise in eastern Europe through a 'merger' with capitalism at the expense of full-blooded 'socialism' would condemn the experiment in advance. Those advocating it could hardly fail to be dubbed revisionists and deviationists – and not in Peking alone.

If we assume that, so long as the bloc can maintain normal trading relations with the West, the USSR is not interested on economic grounds in changing the *status quo*, we are left with the question whether the international scene contains any political features that might induce, or indeed compel, the USSR to adopt a more accommodating attitude. In short, we must discuss China. There has long been a train of thought in Germany, to which Adenauer was the most important subscriber, holding that the growing threat of China on the eastern flank of the USSR would oblige the Kremlin to make concessions to the West. This belief formed part of the 'policy of strength', which we have already considered, and was used to enjoin patience upon the electorate in the Federal Republic.

It is, of course, true that, since Adenauer's retirement, tension has greatly increased between the two leading Communist powers and that doctrinal disagreements have been fed by border clashes. It does not follow, however, that this is likely to promote reunification. There are two arguments pointing in the opposite direction. The first is that, as indicated above, the USSR cannot afford, because of the Chinese challenge, to take major steps in the international field which would seem to depart from Communist orthodoxy. The second is that the greater the threat to the eastern frontiers of the USSR, the more reluctant she will become to have her western frontier exposed, or to lose the relative stability in central Europe which is implicit in the *status quo*. Whatever the long-term advantages to peace and security in Europe that reunification may bring, the immediate prospect of recreating in central Europe a structure resembling, however superficially, that which obtained from 1919 to 1933 cannot look very reassuring. Yet without envisaging a partly disarmed Germany, such as was the Weimar Republic, flanked on the east by states which would have, as after 1919, some degree of genuine independence, it is hard to see how reunification could come about or how it would be an improvement on the present situation.

To state this is not to imply that the author in any way accepts Communist propaganda suggesting that neo-Nazi and revanchist tendencies are prevalent in the Federal Republic. At this point, however, we are trying to use Communist spectacles and we must assume that Russians, even if they do not believe all the exaggerations of their own propaganda, do retain some fear of a reunited Germany.

Brandt, with his usual sagacity, has shown that he neither cherishes unduly sanguine hopes of salvation coming via Peking, nor intends any rash steps designed to bring this about. He has written that, while taking cognizance of Communist disagreements, 'we are going a long way in order to be fair to

16

the role of the Soviet Union and not to give the impression that we are speculating on differences of opinion in the Communist camp. Thus we have rejected taking any initiative as far as relations with the People's Republic of China are concerned. Nor have we pursued the possibility of formalizing our far-from-insignificant trade relations with China.'[15] If global tensions and antagonisms were to reach a crisis, confronting the USSR with the alternative of making major concessions to Germany or risking an alignment between the West and China – surely a crisis which sane statesmanship would exert itself to the utmost to avoid – the initiative would not lie with Germany, but with the USA. It is therefore encouraging to note that the foreign policy of the Federal Republic does not seem to be banking on developments of this kind, with their connotations of international blackmail and imminent nuclear holocaust.

When we turn from the probable attitude of the USSR to that of the USA, we observe that American foreign policy since the end of the war has never shown less inclination than is now the case to embark on 'brinkmanship' for the sake of German reunification, or indeed for any other cause. Not only is American attention concentrated on disengagement from South-East Asia, but it is also apparent that the sense of 'world mission' which once prevailed has been chastened by the war in Vietnam. The era of Pax Americana, if indeed it existed, is well and truly over. It is difficult to conceive of any circumstances, short of unprovoked aggression against Berlin, which would at the present juncture induce the USA to adopt a warlike posture in Europe.

What of other members of the Western Alliance? As we have seen, when the Federal Republic joined it, her NATO allies undertook to pursue the aim of reunification by peaceful means and, until that day came, to regard her as the sole representative of Germany. This commitment was sincerely undertaken and it may be claimed that, at least in London and Washington, efforts were made to give effect to it even at times when a policy of *immobilisme* made Bonn a reluctant partner in the enterprise. No doubt a reaffirmation of good intentions would be forthcoming today in all NATO capitals, if the Federal Republic requested it. But the same answer would not necessarily be made if the question were addressed to the man in the street, instead of to his government.

It is difficult to explain why this should be so without doing injustice to the Federal Republic, which since 1949 had followed an invariably moderate and prudent course in her foreign relations and given no grounds for supposing that a tide of aggressive nationalism would be likely in the foreseeable future to sweep the German people off their feet. It will be recalled that the NPD, the only party in the federal elections of 1969 with a programme demanding a more independent foreign and defence policy, subject to fewer international restrictions, polled no more than 4·3 per cent of the votes and failed to secure a seat in the *Bundestag*. The other parties favoured some variant of the policies consistently pursued in these fields since the Federal Republic gained her freedom of action. In so far as it is possible to gauge the mood of young people in the Federal Republic, they are even less disposed towards international adventures than their elders.

Support for this reassuring view can be found in the declining political importance of the organizations of Germans expelled since the war from lost territories, for whom normalization of relations with eastern Europe would virtually mean permanent exclusion from their native soil. The strongest of these organizations (known as *Landsmannschaften*) represent the expellees from East Prussia, Silesia and the Sudetenland. They are linked in the Federation of Expellees (*BVD*), which claims a membership of 2·5 million; collective membership of all *Landsmannschaften*, including children of the original expellees, is substantially greater. It is clear, however, that for many members their organization fulfils a social rather than a political purpose. The decline of Right Radicalism in its former areas of strength in Lower Saxony and Schleswig-Holstein shows that the refugees in the north have been successfully integrated. Although

Dr Linus Cather, the first Chairman of the *BVD* from 1949 to 1959, has joined the *NPD*, the efforts of its leader, von Thadden, to attract large numbers of expellees with his more assertive foreign policy seem to have met with little success.

In 1950 the *BVD* and representatives of all *Landsmann-schaften*, meeting at Stuttgart, adopted an Expellees' Charter, which renounced 'all thought of revenge and retaliation', while demanding that the 'right to our native land be recognized'. In this document their demand for 'the establishment of a United Europe, in which the nations may live free from fear and force', appeared for the first time. This hope that the problem of the expellees will ultimately disappear when all frontier barriers fall in Europe continues to be the official policy of these pressure groups; but in the meantime they remain opposed to giving to the existing borders the hall-mark of legal recognition. The gradual movement of the *SPD* in this latter direction led early in 1969 to an estrangement between the party and the Chairman of the *BVD*, Reinhold Rehs, who had sat in the *Bundestag* as *SPD* member for a constituency in Schleswig-Holstein. When it became clear that Rehs would not be adopted as *SPD* candidate in the 1969 election, the *CDU* made him the offer of a supposedly safe seat in Lower Saxony. Rehs accordingly changed his party, but failed to hold the seat in September, in spite of his prominent position and the publicity which the episode attracted.

With right-wing extremism at a low ebb throughout the Federal Republic, it is not easy to explain why, outside Germany, enthusiasm for reunification in western Europe seems, if anything, to be declining. Part of the explanation is no doubt to be found in the economic achievements of both parts of Germany and the reputation of the German people for hard work and organizing ability. In the face of these virtues, German assurances of their intention to lead international lives of blameless moderation and co-operation fail to carry complete conviction. Not long ago a Gallup poll was held in Britain in which the question was asked: 'Which country, France, Germany or

Britain, do you think has the most powerful voice in the world today?' In the answers Germany was easily first with 34 per cent, France trailing behind with 25 per cent. When the same question was repeated with the addition of the proviso, 'Looking ahead five years', Germany came further ahead with 45 per cent; Britain, as runner-up, scored only 21 per cent.

If these figures accurately represent what people think at a time when the population of the Federal Republic already exceeds that of Britain, it is not difficult to see why there should be apprehensions about the results of adding on 17 million industrious and disciplined Germans beyond the Elbe. Professor Kaiser, who has provided figures showing the comparative economic standing of a reunited Germany in the world, comments:

> Just as West Germany is the second industrial power in the East. . . . A reunified Germany would not . . . simply be the sum of two existing states. She would occupy an entirely new category – that of a nation whose power fell short of that of the two super-powers but considerably ahead (except for the possession of nuclear weapons) of Europe's traditional great powers like Britain and France.[16]

It may be objected that, if reunification comes about as a result of negotiation between East and West – and short of war there is no other way – it will be hedged about with stipulations designed to restrict any expansive tendencies and to prevent the course of events from following that which disturbed Europe between the wars. There remains, however, the question put so pithily by Mr Macmillan in the House of Commons in 1955: 'If Germany is to be neutral and armed, who is to keep her neutral? If she is to be neutral and disarmed, who is to keep her disarmed?' The question is no easier to answer today; indeed the unforeseen consolidation of the GDR has made it harder. Taking the role of devil's advocate, one might discount, in part, the exemplary behaviour of the Federal Republic, on the ground that she is not in every respect a sovereign state and is still dependent on her principal allies both for the defence of Berlin and for the attainment of reunification. Full independence and sovereignty will come when Berlin is once more the capital of a united Reich; only then will German foreign policy be truly its own.

Before the bar of history, evidence of past good conduct can never serve to dispel all doubts. The statesmanship of Stresemann and the euphoria of Locarno may have briefly held back, but did not divert, the tide of events which culminated in 1939. The historian cannot evade the issue by ascribing successive disasters to some irremediable defect in the German national character; to do so is to overlook patterns of geography and ethnography in central and eastern Europe. But with hindsight he can see that the German Empire fitted into the European mosaic only as long as it also contained the Russian and Austro-Hungarian Empires. After 1917–18 the comment of Ludwig Dehio on the Treaty of Versailles applies: 'Within the narrow framework of the weakened European system, the great German problem could be solved neither by severity, nor by kindness.'[17] The comment is just, even though one may regret that too much severity was used with Stresemann and too much kindness with Hitler. Hitler's war solved nothing; the struggle between East and West for the soul and the living space of Germany has merely continued on a new basis, namely that of partition. The enduring predicament is not changed by our refusal to recognize the present expedient as permanent.

If allied peoples – or, worse still, their governments – say or imply that the partition of Germany is likely to be of indefinite duration, what effect is this likely to have on the Germans themselves, or at least on the West Germans, who can express themselves freely and organize themselves politically? Some evidence has already been quoted to suggest that a great majority approaches this problem in a sober, rational spirit and that the incitements of the extremists have won little support in the face of this attitude. On the other hand, public opinion is notoriously changeable; there can be no guarantee that the state of mind prevailing in Germany today will last as long as partition lasts. One may ask oneself how well it would withstand a prolonged recession in Germany, or a global 'horse-trade' between the super-powers which accepted the *status quo* in Europe as preferable to the risky attempt to alter it.

It is realized in the Federal Republic that the policy of strength, mainly associated with the *CDU*, has failed and that much irredeemable time has been lost. If the policy of conciliation is now tried and also proves to be in vain, a certain backlash could scarcely be avoided. The effect of this would be the more severe if it were felt in the Federal Republic that the cause of reunification had ceased to command the support of her friends and allies. Brandt has written, 'It may be decisive for the future of democracy in our country that our nation not be left to believe in a miracle-to-come, a belief which one day would be frustrated or even turn into a bitter feeling that our friends have let us down.'[18] It would indeed be tragic if the indifference of the other Western powers contributed to the emergence of a harsh nationalism in the Federal Republic, which does not exist today, so transforming Soviet propaganda about revanchism into a self-fulfilling prophecy. Much will depend on the statesmanship displayed within the Western Alliance and on the degree of responsibility shown by the *CDU/CSU* in the unfamiliar role of opposition party.

One cause of understandable impatience in the Federal Republic arises from fear of the enduring effect of brainwashing on the young generations in the GDR exposed to mass media and an educational system permeated with Marxism–Leninism. Some encouragement can, perhaps, be derived from the sturdy resistance of young minds in Czechoslovakia to twenty years of subjection to the Soviet brand of orthodoxy. It must be remembered, however, that the Czechs have behind them a long history of defending their culture and traditions against alien imposition. The history of that part of Germany which now forms the GDR has been different; moreover no one living there who is now under forty can have any recollection of a system permitting independence of thought and expression. Many of the qualities that make Germans good citizens make them poor material for insubordination. Stalin may have been right when he said that Communism would fit Germany as 'a saddle fitted a cow'; but the evidence is inconclusive.

Abandoning these speculations, we must return to the hard realities faced by the new *SPD/FDP* coalition and the policies designed by Brandt and Scheel (Foreign Minister and *FDP* leader) to deal with them. First and most important is the determination not to concentrate either on *Ostpolitik* or on *Deutschlandpolitik*, but to use a trident, of which the central prong represents *rapprochement*, if that is possible, with the USSR. Signature of the non-proliferation treaty (*Atomsperrvertrag*) was a first attempt to sweeten the atmosphere. The reaction in the USSR to the new coalition was cautiously favourable and Brezhnev welcomed what he called a 'more realistic trend' in Bonn, saying he was 'ready to respond' to signs that the GFR recognized 'the real state of affairs' in Europe. This led to the signature in Moscow of the agreement on mutual renunciation of the use or threat of force, first mooted in December 1966, by the old coalition. Ratification in Bonn awaits the outcome of four-power talks on access to West Berlin.

Secondly, Brandt expressed hopes of talks with Poland and, interviewed for *The Times* on 2 November 1969, said 'European stability can only be brought about if Germans and Poles learn to live with each other in the way that the Germans and French have now learned . . .' An opening had been provided by a speech made in May 1969 by Gomulka, who proposed that the Federal Republic agree to recognize the finality of the Oder-Neisse frontier, which, according to traditional Bonn policy, must await a peace treaty. As these rivers form the frontier between Poland and the GDR, which has already recognized it, Gomulka's demand for further recognition implied a certain lack of confidence in Ulbricht's long-term future. The Federal Republic reached agreement with Poland on the inviolability of the latter country's western frontier in November 1970. One

23

wonders whether Brandt was able to turn the Polish trade deficit with the GFR to his advantage in the negotiations!

Poland and the GFR have very little in common, apart from mistrust of Bonn and a firm intention of keeping the hatches battened down at home. If relations between Bonn and Warsaw further improve, it will be more difficult for Ulbricht not to come into line, especially if Brandt remains on good terms with Moscow. Whether the Russians want *détente* on this scale must be open to doubt. Making the large assumption that they do, one may peer a little further into the obscurity and guess that next on the agenda will be the sixteen points of practical co-operation originally proposed to Stoph by Kiesinger. Before this stage arrives, however, there will certainly have been some hard bargaining about recognition. Here Brandt made his position clear at the outset: 'If there exist two states in Germany, they are not foreign countries to each other; their relations with each other can only be of a special nature.' He emphasized the point by renaming the responsible minister in his government 'Minister for Internal German Relations'. But Ulbricht made it plain in his draft treaty of 18 December 1969, that he would not concede Brandt's point without a struggle, in which the support of the USSR seems sure to be invoked.

For Ulbricht the question is by no means one of prestige alone. If he admits that the two Germanies form part of the same nation with a common past, he cannot logically bar the way to a common path into the future. Nor can he, with consistency, prevent human contacts of the kind that bind together peoples with the same heritage. On the other hand, he represents the smaller and weaker of the two parts of Germany and he must fear that the larger part will act as a magnet, because of its greater wealth and the escape it offers from the suffocating atmosphere of Communist orthodoxy. It is as if the boys of Dotheboys Hall woke up to find that a modern permissive school had opened next door. For Squeers–Ulbricht to relax discipline too far would spell the end of Dotheboys Hall.

There is another phase of negotiation, which may yet emerge from the realm of speculation, though at present excluded by Ulbricht's draft treaty. This is the project for a German statute (*Deutschlandstatut*) between the two Germanies, which featured in the *FDP*'s election programme and has, in addition, been outlined in a book by Dr W. W. Schuetz, Chairman of the Council for Indivisible Germany (*Kuratorium Unteilbares Deutschland*).[19] Of Schuetz's fifteen items, some of the more detailed ones are similar to those announced by Kiesinger in April 1967 and subsequently communicated to Stoph. Others have a more general and political character. For example, the first two would require each party to the statute to recognize that the other is not a foreign country, though each effectively administers its own territory. Both would respect human rights, renounce the use of force in external relations and adhere to the basic principles of the charter of the United Nations (to which neither at present belongs). In internal administration both parties would accentuate what is common to their existing legal, social and educational systems and join to set up mixed commissions in Berlin to adjust their policies and plot a course towards eventual unity.

An interim arrangement of this kind is not going to please lawyers; in international law it would have much of the imprecision and incoherence that marks the structure of the British Commonwealth; but it would provide a framework within which 'togetherness', which has been so painfully lacking for the past twenty-five years, could revive and expand. If lawyers seek precedents, they might look for them in the relations between some of the members of the *Deutscher Bund* during the period from 1815 to 1866. Whatever the modalities of the process of growing together, the one thing that is certain about it is that, if it is peaceful, it will be slow, as the resistance and inertia of the powerful *SED* bureaucracy in the GDR is gradually overcome and the post-war *élite* there comes to terms with new developments. There will be no sound of trumpets, at which the walls of Jericho fall down flat; rather there will be the long laborious years during which bridges are built, both literally and figuratively.

All this will require a great deal of patience in the Federal Republic. There is some realization of this, but perhaps not as much as is necessary. In the year before the upheaval in Czechoslovakia the West German historian, Professor Werner Conze, wrote a survey of reunification, which was circulated by Inter Nationes. In this he wrote that, after the Adenauer era, 'there followed a reaction of disappointment, which nowadays finds expression in such silly remarks, for instance, as that we shall probably still not have achieved reunification even in twenty years time. . . . It is an absurd idea to think that we in Germany can still be placed in the same position after ten or twenty years, while world conditions continue to drift further away from the situation of 1945.' It may be desirable for those who are inclined to regard a period of twenty years' waiting as absurd to look back at the history of the nineteenth century. There were major changes of conditions in Europe and some of these, such as the Crimean War, the defeat of Austria at the hands of Prussia and the creation of the Reich, involved powers which had partitioned Poland. Yet, after the last-mentioned of these events had come about, Polish patriots still had to wait nearly fifty years before their country was reunited. Let T. S. Eliot have the last word:

> *I said to my soul, be still, and wait without hope*
> *For hope would be hope for the wrong thing; wait without love*
> *For love would be love of the wrong thing; there is yet faith*
> *But the faith and the love and the hope are all in the waiting.*

References

[1] A. NUTTING, 'Disarmament, Europe and Security', *International Affairs*, vol. 36, no. 1 (1960).

[2] F. H. HARTMANN, *Germany between East and West* (New York, Prentice-Hall, 1965).

[3] K. ADENAUER, *Memoirs (1945–53)* (Stuttgart, Deutsche Verlags-Anstalt, 1965).

[4] Ibid.

[5] Ibid.

[6] K. ADENAUER, *Memoirs (1959–63)* (Stuttgart, Deutsche Verlags-Anstalt, 1968).

[7] H. KROLL, *Botschafter in Belgrad, Tokio and Moskau* (Köln, Kiepenhauer und Witsch, 1967).

[8] Ibid.

[9] R. V. BURKS, 'The Decline of Communism in Czechoslovakia', *Studies in Comparative Communism*, vol. 2, no. 1 (1969).

[10] W. BRANDT, *A Peace Policy for Europe* (London, Weidenfeld & Nicolson, 1969).

[11] W. BRANDT, 'German Policy Towards the East', *Foreign Affairs* (Apr. 1968).

[12] R. V. BURKS, op. cit.

[13] W. BRANDT, op. cit.

[14] K. KAISER, *German Foreign Policy in Transition* (London, Oxford University Press, 1968).

[15] W. BRANDT, op. cit.

[16] K. KAISER, op. cit.

[17] L. DEHIO, *Germany and World Politics in the 20th Century* (London, Chatto & Windus, 1959).

[18] W. BRANDT, op. cit.

[19] W. W. SCHUETZ, *Antipolitik* (Köln, Kiepenhauer und Witsch, 1969).

2 West German Democracy

R. B. TILFORD

The crucial long-term issue on the West German political scene concerns the viability of German liberal democracy. It is therefore around this issue that this chapter on domestic German politics is orientated. Has German democracy since the Second World War been successful? If so, how does one account for this success? Or are there reservations about the extent of the success? If so, what are they?

The second German experiment in liberal democracy has now lasted over twenty years since 1949, when the Federal Republic of Germany was founded. In terms purely of length of life, it has already improved on the first experiment, the Weimar Republic, which lasted only from 1919 to 1933, when it was succeeded by the National Socialist dictatorship, to whose emergence its own weaknesses had contributed.

It has been fashionable among German political writers to express their views about the stability or fragility of West German liberal democracy in the terms 'Bonn is not Weimar'[1] or 'Is Bonn Weimar after all?'[2] Limited historical comparisons, such as that between Bonn and Weimar, risk blurring the necessarily longer historical, as well as international, perspective. However, a brief comparison of the setting in which parliamentary government operated during the two eras may be fruitful for an understanding of contemporary West German democracy.

28

Bonn and Weimar

One of the many causes of the failure of Weimar democracy was, in the view of many critics, the Weimar Constitution, which has been criticized for being 'too democratic', too idealistic. For instance, it placed no limitation on the activities of political parties whose manifest aim was the disruption and abolition of the parliamentary democratic system; this freedom was exploited by the Nazis, the Communists and also by the German National People's (Conservative) Party (*Deutschnationale Volkspartei*). The electoral system – unqualified proportional representation – led to a splintering of political parties, the presence of many parties in the *Reichstag* and made it difficult to form stable governments. There was extensive parliamentary control over the executive; votes of no-confidence were commonplace – the succession of some twenty governments in the space of fourteen years was partly a result of this. The Constitution also provided for a President elected by popular vote and armed with far-reaching 'emergency' powers, which many later writers consider to have been abused and so to have helped undermine Weimar democracy. It attempted unsuccessfully to wed the representative (Anglo-Saxon) and plebiscitary traditions of democracy – the popular election of the President being a manifestation of the latter tradition.

The West German Basic Law (*Grundgesetz*), which provides for a broadly similar political system to the Weimar Republic, is a far more cautious document, implying much more scepticism about the democratic instincts and behaviour of the German politicians and electorate. In some ways it was little more than a reaction against what were considered to be the weaknesses of the Weimar Constitution. One observer says of it, for instance, that it was 'framed by old men who remembered Weimar and had no confidence in man as a political animal'.[3]

Reacting against the licence granted to undemocratic parties by the Weimar Constitution, the framers of the Basic Law provided for a ban on parties 'which, according to their aims and

29

the behaviour of their members, seek to impair or abolish the free and democratic basic order'. Under this provision, two parties, the Socialist Reich Party (*Sozialistische Reichspartei*) and the Communist Party (*Kommunistische Partei Deutschlands or KPD*), have been banned by the Federal Constitutional Court (*Bundesverfassungsgericht*), while in recent years there has been much talk about the possibility of banning the extreme right-wing National Democratic Party (*National-demokratische Partei Deutschlands or NPD*).

The electoral system was modified in two main ways.[4] While still fully proportional in its practical working, half of the members of the *Bundestag* are now directly elected by, and represent, constituencies. It was hoped that this would strengthen the links between the electorate and parliament and increase understanding and support for the parliamentary system. A measure with more immediately obvious results was the introduction of the '5 per cent hurdle' clause, under which a party either has to win 5 per cent of the total vote, or win three constituencies outright before it is entitled to any representation in the *Bundestag*. This clause was aimed at splinter parties and the proliferation of small parties which were such a burden on parliamentary and governmental processes during the Weimar period. The number of parties in the *Bundestag* has in fact fallen from eleven, after the 1949 election, to three, since the 1961 election. One by one, the smaller parties have fallen below the 5 per cent mark or have been swallowed up by one of the two larger parties, the Christian Democrats (*Christlich-Demokratische Union or CDU*) and the Social Democrats (*Sozialdemokratische Partei Deutschlands or SPD*). The third party still represented in the *Bundestag*, the Free Democrats (*Freie Demokratische Partei or FDP*), who have played a significant part as the minor coalition partner in a number of governments, fell dangerously near the dividing line in the 1969 election, when its share of the vote dropped to 5·7 per cent. The controversial extreme right-wing National Democrats were kept out of the *Bundestag* by the fact that they failed by a small margin to reach the 5 per cent mark. If present trends continue, a two-party system seems the likely result. There is little doubt that the sharp decrease in the number of parties – a development for which constitutional provisions are only partly responsible – has made a significant contribution to the stability of the political system, rendering the formation of governments and their maintenance in power a much less chancy business than in the Weimar Republic.

Only two West German governments, at federal level, have failed to complete their four-year term. Of these two cases, only the collapse, in 1966, of the coalition of Christian Democrats and Free Democrats, formed a year previously, and eventually re-placed by the Grand Coalition of the two major parties (Christian and Social Democrats), can be termed a major governmental crisis. Despite the fact that under the present electoral system the number of parties has been reduced to three and may well be reduced still further to two in the future, there is still a persistent lobby in favour of a simple majority electoral system on the British model. This would ensure absolute majorities for single parties, it is argued, and eliminate the instability which might result from continuing coalition government.

Under the Basic Law the position of the President (*Bundespräsident*) has been weakened and that of the Chancellor (*Bundeskanzler* – the equivalent of the British Prime Minister) strengthened. The President's functions are now largely cere-monial. He is no longer elected by popular vote, but rather by a special representative assembly consisting of the *Bundestag* and an equal number of delegates of the *Landtage* (regional parliaments). The Chancellor's position *vis-à-vis* the rest of the government has also been strengthened, in that he is now em-powered by the Basic Law to 'determine the guide-lines of policy', in other words, he may overrule his ministers. Adenauer, in fact, sometimes ignored them. More significantly, the executive's position with regard to the legislature was also strength-ened by placing obstacles in the way of bringing down governments too easily. The principal obstacle is the 'constructive vote of no-confidence' under which the *Bundestag* can only pass a vote of no-confidence in a Chancellor if it simultaneously agrees on his successor. This is intended to inhibit the practice, common in the Weimar Republic (when the Nazis and the Communists once combined for this purpose), of governments being brought down by a temporary coalition of heterogeneous interest with insufficient common ground to form a government themselves.

The Chancellor's position, in theory at any rate, is greatly strengthened by this measure. The term *Kanzlerdemokratie* (Chancellor Democracy) coined in the 1950s, may be an indication of the extent to which the West German political system is weighted in favour of the Chancellor, though here it must be added, particularly in the light of the mixed experiences of the subsequent Chancellors, Kiesinger and Erhard, that Konrad Adenauer's personality and individual governing style, as well as a variety of political and cultural factors, were almost certainly as important as, if not more important than, the Chancellor's constitutional position.

Nevertheless, a strong Chancellor, like the reduction in the number of parties, is one of the factors that, at least in the 1950s, made for political stability in post-war West Germany. In a country whose inhabitants have traditionally been used to, and seem to need, a strong executive, it was probably a wise move to make constitutional provision for a strong Chancellor, at least as a transitional measure until liberal democracy has put down deeper roots in Germany. The executive, according to this view, had to be strong enough to exercise a protective and tutelary function, to watch over the establishment of democracy and to ward off possible threats to it, until the emergence of a positive commitment to the political system, as opposed to a passive acceptance of it, rendered this 'educative' function of the executive unnecessary. Adherents of this view claim that one of the mistakes of the Weimar Constitution was too abrupt a transition from very little to a great deal of parliamentary control over government. Giving the Chancellor a strong position would provide for a more gradual transition after the Second World War. However, it is arguable whether the Chancellor's position is any stronger than, say, that of the British Prime Minister and it would thus be as well to guard against the assumption that the Basic Law was pandering to a German weakness for a 'strong man' or continuing a tradition of 'revolutions from above'.

It is perhaps ironic that these constitutional devices, aimed at safeguarding democracy, eloquent as they are of a degree of mistrust of the democratic instincts of politicians and electorate alike, are also criticized for having played a part in inhibiting the growth of democratic attitudes and behaviour. It is argued both that they tend to aid the maintenance of the gap between the rulers and ruled which is traditionally wider in Germany than in the English-speaking liberal democracies and also that they have assisted the development of what militant student critics – the so-called 'extra-parliamentary opposition' (*Ausserparlementarische Opposition* or *ApO*) – termed the 'oligarchies' and 'cartels' which run the country. To rectify this, these critics – and in this they are joined by the extreme right-wing National Democrats – advocate measures to decrease the gap between rulers and ruled (for instance, the direct election of, and increased powers for, the President, and the holding of referenda), some of which are precisely the measures which the framers of the Basic Law considered to have contributed to the collapse of Weimar democracy.

A further institutional innovation designed to ensure the stability of the new political system was the Federal Constitutional Court, whose broad function is to see that the Basic Law is observed. This court, the West German equivalent of the American Supreme Court, was attacked earlier in the life of the Federal Republic on the grounds that it tended to perpetuate the legalistic approach to politics characteristic of German political development; in this view the legislature in Germany is not the final arbiter of political differences, whose decision can only be changed by the voters, but merely a forum where arguments may be aired before eventually being submitted to the Constitutional Court. One effect of the 'judicialization of political dynamics', so this criticism runs, may be a retardation of the general acceptance of a body of political, as opposed to legalistic, 'rules of the game'. However, in a country with a great legal tradition it is hardly surprising that the weight of this tradition should be used to underpin and 'legitimize' the new and fragile political system. Experience has shown that the institution of the Constitutional Court is one of the most highly esteemed of West German institutions and that it has probably contributed to the gradually growing commitment to the political system.

Conditions of Democracy: Weimar

While recognizing the importance of constitutions, most interpreters of German political history now tend to emphasize other factors in their analyses of the relative fragility and stability of the Weimar Republic and the Federal Republic. It is maintained that after the First World War there was a lack of congruence between the political norms established by the Constitution on the one hand, and political traditions, attitudes and behaviour on the other. Reduced to a simple formula: Weimar Germany was a democracy with insufficient democrats and a republic with insufficient republicans.

In 1919 many Germans felt that 'Western' democracy had been foisted on them as a result of a conspiracy between the Allied victor powers and their own 'traitorous' democratic politicians. This 'stab in the back' legend (*Dolchstoss-Legende*) fostered the idea that Germany had been undefeated in the field and that she had been 'sold down the river' by her own democratically inclined politicians – henceforth to be called 'November traitors' by many – who preferred defeat in war to victory, as long as defeat brought with it a democratic political system. For many Germans – towards the end of the Weimar Republic it was probably the majority – the new political system was associated with defeat in war, with betrayal and ignominy, and

34

they rejected it as a foreign imposition and in essence 'un-German'. The economic and social catastrophes which beset the Weimar Republic – the rampant inflation of 1923 and the Depression of 1929–32 – were also strong factors working against the popular acceptance of the system.

Weimar democracy was, in the words of one eminent German political scientist, a 'hasty improvization'.[5] Evolution towards parliamentary government had been very slow. There was little experience of genuine representative government. Liberal democracy had not come by popular demand but ironically at the instigation of the wartime military leadership, which was tactically, but certainly not democratically, motivated. The majority of Germans, despite occasional dissatisfaction in the labour movement and unrest among Catholics, had, it seemed, been content with the authoritarian political regime of Bismarckian and Wilhelmine Germany, which had not granted them a full participant role in the political process and therefore not helped prepare them for life in a democratic society, but under which Germany had prospered to become a world power and a leading industrial nation with a model system of compulsory social insurance. Germany before the First World War has been described as the 'best-administered and worst-governed' state in western Europe. This may be true if we understand by 'worst-governed', 'least democratically governed'. The fact remains that most Germans were not enthusiastic about changing the political system, even if they had become disenchanted with the Kaiser by the end of the First World War. The authoritarian state, with the political parties relegated to the ante-room of the governmental process, instead of participating directly in it, was acceptable to them.

The parties which formed the first Weimar government – the (Catholic) Centre Party (*Zentrum*), the Social Democrats and the small (Liberal) German Democratic Party (*Deutsche Demokratische Partei*) – had no experience of government. They were used only to opposition and were not conditioned to think of the possibility of assuming power. Saddled with the

35

responsibility of power, they were unsure of themselves and uncertain how to behave in their new roles. There was also little experience in the art of compromise – the essence of parliamentary government, particularly where the electoral system tends to make coalition government necessary. Discussion, debate and conflict, the articulation of differing political and social interests, are the central features of representative democracy. But, if the system is to be coherent, such debate, argument and conflict must take place on the foundation of agreement on the 'rules of the game', of a consensus of opinion about the validity of the political system itself. Such consensus was lacking in the Weimar Republic. The system itself was under attack from major political groupings on the Right and on the Left. Party-political argument on the basis of fundamental ideological cleavage can promote the disintegration of democratic political systems and it can be persuasively maintained that this is what happened to the Weimar Republic.

The year 1918, which marked a political revolution in Germany in the sense that the system of government was radically changed, was scarcely a social revolution. The senior levels in three key institutions – the military, the bureaucracy and the judiciary – continued to be staffed to a large extent by members of the upper class, who were monarchical in political orientation, who had been used to being regarded as the political and social *élite* and who resented the idea that they should now subordinate themselves to a political executive which derived its support from political parties, for whom, in company with many of their countrymen, they had scant respect. The new democratic rulers made little systematic attempt to democratize these institutions, whose composition remained largely representative of the pre-democratic, authoritarian, monarchical order. In the early years of the Weimar Republic, economic and social conditions were so unsettled and, at times, chaotic that even the Social Democrats were forced – or thought they were forced – to rely for the maintenance of some semblance of order on the old bureaucracy and military; that is, on elements at best lukewarm in their tolerance of the democratic system and often hostile to it. This initial compromise with social and political forces which were at root inimical to the development of parliamentary democracy and which occupied key positions enabling them to hinder the implementation of democratic constitutional norms, was to prove a major handicap to Weimar democracy. This is vividly illustrated by the behaviour of the army, which managed to function as a 'state within a state' and whose loyalty to the regime was not assured. Only a thorough-going social revolution, which would have removed the traditional authoritarian *élites* from their positions of influence, could, it is held by many political historians, have created the conditions in which the new political system could have flourished.

Conditions of Democracy: Bonn

The conditions under which the Federal Republic came into being, as well as the greater degree to which the ideological, sociological and economic requisites of liberal democracy have been present, have favoured a more successful establishment of a liberal–democratic system since 1949 than was the case after the First World War.

The military defeat was absolutely unambiguous; there was no scope for a 'stab in the back' legend. The new regime was not associated with alleged betrayal. The lack of association between defeat and the new regime was facilitated by the lapse of four years between the end of the war in 1945 and the establishment of the new regime in 1949, a time-lag that was sufficient for the true nature of the Nazi regime, in particular the massacre of the Jews, to be revealed. As a result, Fascism was widely discredited – which the authoritarian regime at the end of the First World War was not. Nor was the alternative of Communism acceptable to the West Germans (let alone the Western occupying powers). Any sympathies for Communism had almost certainly been dissipated by the sometimes brutal invasion and occupation of East and Central Germany, as well as by the increasingly apparent repressive nature of the Communist regime in the part of Germany that was to become the German Democratic Republic. In addition, it was hardly likely that the many years of Nazi anti-Soviet propaganda would not leave their mark (indeed it was not long before Hitler's anti-Soviet tirades were, in the eyes of not a few Germans, to be to some extent vindicated by the enlistment of the Federal Republic on the side of the West in the Cold War against the Communist bloc of countries). A democratic regime of the liberal, parliamentary type was, in fact, the only possible choice to be made. In a sense there is an analogy with the Weimar Republic here in that the new regime, if not a foreign import, was watched over and approved by the Allies, who even after 1949 retained powers of intervention in West Germany in the event of their considering the democratic order to be in jeopardy. However, partly for the reasons already discussed, there was little feeling among Germans that it had been imposed on them and they were not hostile to it. The only exception to this in recent years has come from the National Democrats, who have applied the derogatory term *Lizenzparteien* (parties licensed by the Allies) to the three parties represented in the *Bundestag*.

There is, then, a broad consensus of ideological opinion in West Germany in favour of the liberal–democratic political order, which is not under attack from any significant political grouping, even the National Democrats, if they are to be taken at their word and their stated commitment to the democratic order is not questioned. In this respect the Federal Republic is better off than the Weimar Republic, though question-marks still hang over the degree and intensity of commitment to the new system, whether the commitment is positively or negatively (anti-Communist?) motivated, and over the ability of the system to survive an economic crisis.

The Federal Republic is also better off with respect to the sociological requisites of liberal democracy. German society after the First World War was still characterized by the extent to which birth and social class determined access to the *élites*

38

in a number of important spheres. One of the ironic and beneficial achievements of National Socialism, as far as the Federal
Republic is concerned, is that these groups, which had at best
shown a reserved attitude to the Weimar regime, were either
removed or their influence much diminished. The Nazis had
little sympathy for the conservative pre-democratic political
and social *élites*, though they were forced to collaborate with
them in the initial stages of their regime. It was, in fact, from
the officer corps of the military which had been largely hostile
or indifferent to the Weimar regime, and which was still
largely aristocratic in spirit, that the only serious resistance to
the Nazis came. For their part in the attempted assassination of
Hitler in 1944 the officer corps was purged. Many others died
in the war. Those *Junker* (the landed Prussian aristocracy) who
remained were deprived of the economic basis of their social
prestige and political influence through the loss of their
lands, which were for the most part behind the Iron Curtain.
The same was true, though to a lesser extent, of the bureaucracy.

In addition, the top positions in many walks of life during the
Nazi period, including professions in which success had traditionally been linked with social origin and privilege, had been
filled with loyal Nazi officials and supporters, very often of
lower-middle or working-class origin. Although this substituted
political for social privilege, it did have a long-term social
leavening effect. The demise of the old authoritarian *élites*, the
Nazi 'social revolution' and the chaotic disruption of German
life at the end of the war, a disruption in which there were unprecedented opportunities for geographic and social mobility –
all these factors helped lead to a German society after 1945
which, in terms of social equality and social mobility, was far
more 'open' than had earlier been the case and which was for
these reasons more conducive to the establishment of a viable
liberal democracy. This is not to say that serious social inequalities do not remain – the present crisis in the West German
educational system provides plentiful evidence that it does –

39

but simply that social privilege is now a much less important factor than previously.

The end of the German officer corps as an illiberal political force was also facilitated by the fact that the Federal Republic had no armed forces until 1955. In fact, the Basic Law specifically forbade them and a constitutional amendment was necessary before rearmament, which encountered the hostility of a large part of the West German populace, was possible. This hostility is an indication of the extent to which the traditionally high prestige of the military and the penetration of society as a whole by military (and intrinsically illiberal) values had waned. The contrast with the Weimar Republic was marked. After 1949, the new regime was in a position to determine the shape of the new military, to influence its philosophy, and to take measures – examples are the concept of the *Bürger in Uniform* ('democratic citizen in uniform'), the school for *Innere Führung* ('conscience-guided behaviour'), the Parliamentary Commissioner for the Armed Forces – to democratize both the internal structure of the military and its relations with the political leadership.

New and fragile political systems without much support in national traditions and popular attitudes seem especially vulnerable to a variety of external circumstances, of which, with the possible exception of war, fluctuations in economic conditions seem to be the most important. The radicalization of politics – growth in the support of the anti-democratic extremist parties – during the Weimar Republic occurred when economic conditions were at their worst, that is, in 1923, at a time of runaway inflation and large-scale unemployment and between 1929 and 1932, during the Depression, which was also accompanied by widespread unemployment. The almost unbroken economic success of the Federal Republic and the unprecedented national and individual prosperity this has brought have probably been the single most important factor in 'legitimizing' the new regime as far as the citizens of the Federal Republic are concerned. Here, too, Bonn has been more fortunate than Weimar, though, as already indicated, a question-mark remains over the ability of the regime to survive serious economic difficulties. Even the German economic recession of 1966 – an insignificant one in the international comparison – was accompanied by a sharply increased vote in *Land* and local elections for the newly formed National Democrats. It also led to the formation of the Grand Coalition, which, through bringing the two major parties together in the same government and leaving only a numerically insignificant parliamentary opposition, violated one of the principal functions of parliament: to provide an effective opposition which will exercise a measure of control over government.

Nor should the political parties be ignored. As we have seen, the parties during the Weimar period tended to adopt a dogmatic ideological stance, unwilling or unable to exhibit the flexibility and readiness for compromise which is a characteristic of political parties in the Anglo-Saxon countries. They customarily restricted their appeal to a particular socio-economic or socio-cultural group. The blurring of traditional class divisions, other social and cultural changes, as well as the less dogmatically ideological approach of the contemporary parties, have joined with the already mentioned constitutional devices to limit the number of parties and to make possible the 'mass' party, that is, a party which draws its support from a variety of socio-economic and socio-cultural groupings, on the model of the Republicans and Democrats in the United States and, to a lesser extent, the Labour and Conservative parties in Great Britain. The function of the parties as an 'integrating' force in society, that is, in providing a common bond for members of differing socio-economic and socio-cultural groups, is held by some political sociologists to be essential in encouraging mutual toleration of political differences and therefore to be indispensable in any viable liberal democracy. 'Mass' parties, according to this theory, would be particularly important in Germany, a country riven by historical, ideological and religious conflicts to an extent unknown in most English-speaking countries. The

Weimar parties tended to reflect and accentuate these differences. The Christian Democrats, Social Democrats and Free Democrats, on the other hand, act as 'integrating' factors.

The Christian Democrats were the first party to make the transition to a 'mass' party. A new party, led from the early post-war period by Adenauer, the *CDU* was in some ways the successor of the (Catholic) Centre Party of the Wilhelmine and Weimar periods. Indeed the Centre Party, like other denominationally based parties, can in a sense be seen as the precursor of modern 'mass' parties in that it drew its support from all classes: what its voters had in common was their Catholicism. However, the very existence of a political party along strictly denominational lines (traditional in continental European politics) tended to keep historical hostilities alive – official discrimination against Catholics had occurred on a large scale in Bismarck's time – and acted as a barrier to the normal articulation of differing socio-economic interests by the political parties. The Christian Democrats by being the successor not only to the Centre Party but also to a number of smaller parties, including the conservative and largely Protestant German National People's Party, has spread its mantle to embrace both major denominations, though it still draws approximately 70 per cent of its support from Catholics (the West German population is almost evenly divided between Protestants and Catholics), and has fulfilled an important function in making political affiliation less dependent on religious loyalties. The result is that, by German standards, the *CDU* is an extremely heterogeneous party; it draws its support from farmers and rural workers, from the Catholic and Protestant middle class, from Catholic industrial workers and from businessmen and tradesmen; the composition of the *Fraktion* (parliamentary party) reflects this diversity. In the absence of a large body of professional party workers at various levels, the *CDU* needed strong leadership if it was to cohere. Such leadership was supplied by Adenauer, though it is less sure that it has been supplied subsequently.

42

The Social Democrats, the oldest German party and the only one to survive from the Weimar Republic, took longer to develop into a 'mass' party. It is traditionally the party of the industrial working class and did not at first widen its appeal after the founding of the Federal Republic. Nevertheless it is the only party in western Europe and Scandinavia to have increased its share of the vote at every election since the Second World War (1969: *CDU* 46·1 per cent; *SPD* 42·6 per cent). The crucial development in the expansion of the *SPD*'s appeal beyond the working class, apart from sociological changes in the electorate, such as the diminishing number of farmers, was the party's *Godesberger Programm* of 1959, in which it divested itself of the last traces of Marxist ideology, turned its back on national-ization and proclaimed its support for the 'social market economy'. Since that time, the *SPD* has been gradually in-creasing its support among professional people of both denomi-nations and even among voters in the Catholic rural areas. Apart from the increasingly important 'integrative' part played by the *SPD*, it has served the new political system particularly well as a 'loyal' opposition. It was in opposition in the *Bundestag* from 1949 to 1966 and, during that time, the *SPD*'s criticism of government policies was always launched from a position of loyalty to the political system and adherence to constitutional principles. This was in spite of the violent and acrimonious initial opposition to Adenauer's crucial and, at that time, contro-versial policy of rearmament and membership of NATO and West European organizations, which Schumacher, the first post-war leader of the *SPD*, thought would deepen the division of Germany; and despite the treatment received at the hands of Adenauer, which sometimes prompted speculation about whether or not he appreciated the purpose and value of a parlia-mentary opposition. The *CDU*, which was in power con-tinuously from 1949 to 1969, and therefore has no experience of opposition at federal level, now had an opportunity to demonstrate its understanding of, and aptitude for, parlia-mentary opposition.

Political Institutions

The new democratic institutions of the Federal Republic have also survived intact and have functioned adequately for the most part. Some of the most frequent criticisms of West German democracy are those that can be made of the liberal-democratic system wherever it exists. The arrival of 'big government' – the spread of government to all corners of society – and its increasing specialization in modern industrial societies has made government less capable of being comprehended, scrutinized and controlled by the electorate and their representatives in the legislatures, the increase in the power of the executive *vis-à-vis* the legislature, the gap between rulers and ruled, the apparent predominance of 'establishments' or 'ruling oligarchies', the difficulty of citizen-participation in the political decision-making process, the formulation of important political policies and the taking of decisions, as it were in secret, by 'faceless' bureaucrats: all of these ills of modern liberal democracy are present in the English-speaking democracies as well as the Federal Republic. This international phenomenon may, however, have a specifically German dimension. German traditions favour a strong executive and a comparatively weak legislature; Germany has tended to have a highly regarded Civil Service accustomed to the making of policy as well as its implementation (the dictum: 'politics should be left to the experts' clearly belongs in this context) and the attitude to politicians has been correspondingly less favourable. This tends to make political processes more prone to bureaucratization and more distant from the individual than those in the English-speaking countries.

The efficacy of parliament itself and the popular regard in which it is held is one measure of the stability of the parliamentary system. Loewenberg, the author of a recent comprehensive work on the West German parliament, claims that the organization and working methods of the *Bundestag* – the network of parties and parliamentary parties, their executives and working parties, of parliamentary committees and plenary sessions, of senior civil servants and interest-group representatives – is no longer comprehensible to the outsider, nor to a number of Bonn newspaper correspondents, nor even to some members of the *Bundestag*. But, he continues, the *Bundestag* has developed the organizational procedures which it needs in the present political situation. The successful adaptation of the inherited structure of the *Bundestag* to the demands of the changed party system and the new relationship between the executive and parliament have lent the German parliament new vitality. However, the changes involved in this adaptation have not been institutionalized – they depend on informal procedures, norms and agreements between the parliamentary parties which often appear obscure to the public. The interested public is deprived of accurate knowledge of the patterns of behaviour which set the framework for parliamentary activities, and, continues Loewenberg, it is on this knowledge that the long-term survival of parliament depends. He concludes that the legislative activity of the *Bundestag* permit it to exercise significant influence on many sectors of government policy. But since a large part of the legislative work takes place in private, rather than in plenary sittings, it cannot be followed in detail by the public. This permits the *Bundestag* to work impressively from the point of view of the volume and quality of its work – which Loewenberg is quick to acknowledge – but it also means that the public does not know which problems are being debated and what the results of the debate are. The efficiency of the *Bundestag* is inversely proportional to its popular esteem; in one sense it is better than its reputation indicates. The contact between the public and parliament is, according to Loewenberg, more seriously threatened in Germany than in any other country in the Western world. He speaks of an 'underdeveloped function' of the *Bundestag* as a 'representative organ'. In essence what the *Bundestag* illustrates is the international dilemma of reconciling organizational efficiency with democratic claims. As one might expect in Germany, partly because of the specifically German dimension to this dilemma mentioned earlier, the *Bundestag* meets the first of these needs rather better than the second.

West German federalism – the division of political power between the *Bund* (centre) and the *Länder*, which, as well as having their own legislatures (*Landtage*) and governments, are represented in Bonn through the second chamber of the Federal Parliament, the *Bundesrat* – has also functioned so far in keeping with the letter of the Basic Law. Part of the motivation behind the incorporation of the federal structure in the Constitution was the desire of the Western Allies to decentralize political power as a barrier in the way of a possible resurgence of totalitarianism. However, though such decentralization has deep roots in German history, the long-term historical trend, which can be traced from pre-unification days through the Bismarckian and Wilhelmine eras, the Weimar Republic and the Nazi regime, is towards more centralization. Moreover, the general trend in modern industrial societies with advanced technologies towards more centralization, whether in industry and commerce or in government, acts against the federal principle in Germany as elsewhere. And although the *Länder* jealously guard their legislative prerogatives, which are mainly in the spheres of taxation, education and the police, there is little doubt that these prerogatives have undergone a gradual process of erosion, especially in the area of taxation, but more recently also in the sphere of education. In 1969, for instance, the new Social Democrat/Free Democrat government appointed for the first time a Federal Minister of Education, despite the fact that the Federal Government has no legislative powers in the sphere of education. It is in part this process that has led one observer to characterize West German federalism as an 'executive-legislative' federalism, that is, as a type in which there is not a significant division of legislative powers between the *Bund* and *Länder*, which would be the classic type of federalism, but a division between legislative powers on the one hand, which are largely in the hands of the *Bund*, and executive and particularly administrative powers on the other, which are preponderantly

46

in the hands of the *Länder*. In keeping with this, the *Bund* maintains only a small bureaucracy, while the *Länder*, which are responsible for administering most federal legislation in addition to their own, have large bureaucracies.

It is perhaps ironic that at a time when the increasing specialization of government and the consequent remoteness of the individual from the policy-making process has provoked the demand for more citizen-participation (*Mitbestimmung*) in politics including the demand in Britain for a measure of devolution of political power from Westminster to the regions, the trend in Germany, where the demands for 'democratization' have been particularly vociferous, should be towards more centralization. Here it should be emphasized that the *Bundesrat* is an effective guardian in Bonn of the interests of the *Länder*, but scarcely an agency promoting more 'participation'.

Two episodes which put the political institutions of the Federal Republic under some strain and illustrated both negative and positive aspects of West German democracy were the '*Spiegel* affair' and the dispute over the succession to the presidency in 1959. Leading editors of *Der Spiegel*, a highly successful West German news magazine, were arrested in October 1962, at the instigation – as it emerged subsequently – of the then Federal Defence Minister, Strauss. The reason for the arrests was an allegedly treasonable article about a NATO exercise. There was doubt about the legality of the arrests; the Minister of Justice was deliberately kept in ignorance of them; Strauss denied in the *Bundestag* that he was connected with the arrests, only to recant later – under pressure; Chancellor Adenauer said in the *Bundestag* in connection with the *Spiegel* arrests, before a charge had been brought: 'Our country is an abyss of treason'; the *CDU/FDP* coalition nearly collapsed (the Minister of Justice was a Free Democrat); Strauss was forced to resign; the Minister for Internal Affairs, Hocherl, admitted that one of the arrests had been carried out in a manner 'somewhat outside the bounds of legality'. The high-handedness and scant respect for democratic procedures or the law on the part of leading politicians threatened to undermine public confidence in the democratic instincts of their leaders and came near to bringing down the government. However, the institutions of parliamentary democracy, though abused in this case, survived and the affair had some positive results in that the vehemence of the press and popular reaction showed that there was a greater general awareness of the importance of democratic behaviour among West Germans than the conduct of some of their leaders in this affair would indicate.

The prestige of political institutions and offices was also not enhanced by Chancellor Adenauer's behaviour in 1959 over the question of the succession to the Presidency on the death of the first West German President, Professor Heuss. Adenauer at first decided he would put himself up for the presidency; he saw in this office a means of guaranteeing the continuity of his policies. However, when it was made clear to him that the powers of the presidency were extremely limited, and when it seemed likely that his party colleague, Professor Erhard, whom he considered unfit for the office, would follow him as Chancellor, he changed his plan and decided to remain Chancellor. His party, the Christian Democrats, were embarrassed by the behaviour of their leader and decided that would be his last term of office. However, by that time, Adenauer's cavalier treatment of the country's most senior offices had diminished the prestige not only of his government but also of the offices themselves. From the point of view of Adenauer himself, it seems sad that his earlier achievements should tend to be obscured by the frailties of his declining years.

Even these rather disturbing episodes, then, had their encouraging features and contained indications of an increased degree of support among the population for a democratic regime. Public opinion surveys go some way towards substantiating these signs. In 1951, 45 per cent of West Germans still considered the Kaiser's era to have been the best and 42 per cent chose the Nazi era; the corresponding figures for 1963 showed that only 16 per cent still felt Imperial Germany to have been best and only 10 per cent still chose Hitler's Germany, while 66 per cent now believed 'they had never had it so good' as now and to that extent identified themselves with the Federal Republic. Admittedly, the 1963 poll also showed that the Weimar Republic was still very poorly rated, which may be an indication that the acceptance of the Federal Republic depends rather on economic factors than an appreciation of the system of government.

In 1969 one of the crucial tests of the stability of any new parliamentary regime – a smooth change of governing party – was passed when the Social Democrats became the senior governing party for the first time. The time taken to negotiate the new *SPD/FDP* coalition was shorter than for any other government since 1949 and the negotiations were not accompanied by any public unrest, although there was a tendency for a part of the national press (the Springer chain) and of the Bavarian Christian Socialists (the *CSU*) to regress to the type of 'national' opposition that was typical of the Weimar Republic. There may be something in the argument that the smooth change of senior governing party was facilitated to some extent by the fact that the *SPD* first 'proved itself' – i.e. served a kind of governmental apprenticeship – by governing in the Grand Coalition with the *CDU* from 1966 to 1969, during which time some of its ministers, for example Economics Minister Schiller, were conspicuously successful in mastering their ministerial tasks and consequently in persuading even that part of the electorate traditionally hostile to the *SPD*, of its competence to govern.

It is also claimed that the new political system has shown its efficacy and the degree of loyalty it has won in the electorate by the way in which the challenge from the extremist parties, in particular the National Democrats, has, for the time being at any rate, been beaten off. Indeed many foreign observers saw the 'defeat' of the *NPD* at the 1969 Federal Election as the most significant aspect of that election, in that it showed that the German electorate had finally reached 'political maturity'.

49

There is probably some truth in this interpretation of the
NPD's 1969 election performance. But, before reaching hasty
conclusions about the fate of extremist parties, it should be
remembered that the election took place at a time of economic
boom, great consumer prosperity and full employment; that the
NPD was exposed to a government threat of a constitutional ban
during the election campaign, a fact which possibly cast the
'respectability' of the *NPD* in doubt as far as some of its
potential supporters were concerned; that the *NPD* received
over twice as many votes in the 1969 election as it did in 1965;
and that the *NPD* won a mere 1 per cent less of the total vote
cast than the Free Democrats (*NPD*: 4·6 per cent; *FDP*: 5·7 per
cent), yet, as a result of the electoral system, the *NPD* is not
represented in the *Bundestag* at all, while the *FDP*, in contrast,
is not only in the *Bundestag*, but is one of the governing parties.
It is interesting to speculate that if the performances of the two
parties had been reversed and the *NPD* had found its way into
the *Bundestag*, a continuation of the Grand Coalition would
almost certainly have resulted, as a consequence of the refusal
of both the *SPD* and *CDU* to govern with the 'neo-fascist'
National Democrats.

Many observers of German politics claim that membership
and acceptance of the West German regime by its citizens
bears a decidedly formal and passive character.[7] Positive links
to the regime are relatively weak. The opinion surveys reflect an
indifferent, perhaps 'unpolitical', attitude to the West German
regime, very different from the intense identification of Germans
in other eras with Imperial or National Socialist Germany, but
also very different from the rejection of Weimar democracy.
Dutiful compliance with the rules of the constitution, huge
polls at election time (the right to vote is interpreted very much
as a duty), and the concentration of electoral support on the
political parties that are identified with the regime – these traits
may well furnish some evidence of a congruent relationship
between the regime (or the system of government) and the
political culture (that is, the group of attitudes, values and

50

beliefs from which a people's basic political attitudes spring). But they also seem to conceal attitudes which may *apparently* contribute to the stability of the system (a passive, non-participatory electorate which thinks politics should be left to the experts is unlikely to trouble the regime's stability, at least in the short term), but which do not promote the positive commitment to the system which it requires if it is to acquire the kind of 'legitimacy' which will enable it to weather serious storms (a major economic recession, for instance).

The traditional German dictum that the citizen's first duty is to stay a calm (passive?) subject (*Ruhe ist die erste Bürgerpflicht*) still appears to prevail in the Federal Republic. Political demands articulated outside the established formal channels are frowned on, as the public and official reactions to the 'student rebellion' in 1967 and the succeeding years showed. The prevailing desire for stability (the *CDU*'s favourite election slogan was 'No Experiments', *keine Experimente*), and conformity, and the widespread passiveness of the electorate has had two chief effects on the operation of the political system. Firstly, participation in the political policy-making process is left largely to the *élites* in a number of spheres.[8] Secondly, government has remained relatively unencumbered by mass pressures for the satisfaction of conflicting demands. There has been less need to respond to public sentiment than in the Weimar Republic or, for that matter, in present-day Britain. The stability that this facilitates may be fragile, especially if the relative lack of mass pressures leads the government to postpone or neglect urgent measures or reforms. The current controversy over education, described by one writer in a rather dramatic fashion as the German 'educational catastrophe', can be seen in this light. After two decades (1949–69) of *non*-reform (compare what was happening in other West European countries over the same period) and astonishingly little public criticism and pressure, the failings of the educational system became so evident, and, particularly in the university sphere, so crippling,[9] that there has been an explosion of resentment, which, particularly among the educated young in the 'extra-parliamentary' opposition, has tended to turn into a disenchantment with the political system as such.

Allegiance to, and support for, the democratic political regime stands in a rather vexed relationship to the problem of national unity and reunification. In the earlier discussion we saw that, from the point of view of the ideological requisites of stable liberal democracy, Bonn is far better off than Weimar. Whether the situation has also improved from the point of view of the historical and continuing German search for unity and a national identity, whether the replacement of the profound ideological cleavage and confusion of Weimar Germany (which, for all its drawbacks, was *one* Germany) by the clean division into *two* German states embodying distinct ideologies and incorporated into opposing ideological camps ought to be preferred are questions which touch the very roots of what some historians consider to be the cause of German 'political aberration'. By this they usually mean the divergence from the democratic political development of the English-speaking and the other West European countries. The concepts of the nation-state and of democracy, instead of growing side by side and supporting each other, grew apart from each other in the course of the nineteenth century and in the twentieth century have often appeared to be mutually exclusive. The present division of Germany is a particularly vivid illustration of the historical conflict in Germany between these two main fruits of the French Revolution. What are West Germans to prefer? Democracy or national unity? Should they be prepared to sacrifice liberal democracy, or at least accept a dilution of it, in the interests of national unity (reunification), or will they be prepared to sacrifice unity in the interests of the maintenance of liberal democracy in at least the western part of Germany? Put like that the dilemma may seem rather contrived. But the late Karl Jaspers, for one, was in no doubt that this is the essential long-term choice that faces West Germans, and insisted that democracy should be given precedence over national unity.[10] However, the Federal Republic is a *provisional* state pending the reunification of Germany. This is anchored in the Preamble to the Basic Law (the term 'Basic Law' rather than 'Constitution' was chosen to emphasize the provisory nature of the state). Can loyalty and commitment to a provisional state be expected, even if its regime is a democratic one? There is a good case to be made for the argument that a new and fragile political system requires the support of a secure sense of national identity on the part of its citizens. Can this sense of identity be achieved, while in the words of one well-known writer, Hans Magnus Enzensberger, Germans 'live in two halves of a whole that does not exist'?

The Federal Republic has repeatedly claimed – this, too, is anchored in the Basic Law – that it represents *all* Germans (it considers itself the only legitimate German state), and that reunification must be achieved on the basis of the right to self-determination of *all* Germans (which is tantamount to saying 'democracy for all Germans'). For the time being, however, it could be argued that reunification is not a realistic proposition, whatever the Basic Law may say, and that the democratic consensus in West Germany is therefore not troubled by the possibility of any immediate concessions which might have to be made in the interests of national unity. This may be true, but, on the other hand, there is no doubt that the idea of the nation has come to the forefront of discussion again recently in the Federal Republic. There have been more frequent calls for an increase in national consciousness, not merely from the National Democrats, but also from politically far more moderate quarters. In part this stems from disillusionment over the failure of European organizations to provide for the sublimation of national interests in supranational communities. The policy of the *SPD/FDP* coalition, formed in late 1969, towards the German Democratic Republic represents both a response to, and an intensification of, this mood. The policy of Chancellor Brandt and Foreign Minister Scheel is a sharp break with the policies of all previous West German governments. Their policy is characterized on the one hand by the relegation to a position of lower priority of the claim to 'represent all Germans' (for the first time it received no mention in the government policy statement) and of the claim that all Germans should have the 'right to self-determination' (this was mentioned only once), as well as by a greater readiness to recognize the legitimate existence of a second German state, and, on the other hand, by a much heavier emphasis than previously on the idea of the nation as the only strong bond left between Germans in the two Germanies, apart from family links. Brandt has summed up his policy in the phrase 'two German states of one nation' (*zwei deutsche Staaten einer Nation*), a phrase which also puts in a nutshell the dilemma discussed on the last page or two.

In studying the passiveness of the German electorate the 'burnt fingers' motif should not be ignored. The 'total' politicization of the Nazi period – the political penetration of areas of society and individual life not normally considered political, the pressures to show public commitment to National Socialism, etc. – was succeeded by the desire of people who felt they had their 'fingers burnt' to have nothing whatsoever to do with politics, to withdraw into the private sphere. In recent years, however, there have been signs of a revival of a more normal relationship to politics. An interesting facet of the 1969 election campaign, for instance, was the 'references campaign' (*Referenzenkampagne*). Groups of people prominent in public life, particularly in cultural life and the entertainment world, took out large joint advertisements in newspapers and magazines, proclaiming their support for one of the political parties (as it happened, usually for the *SPD*). In so doing, they made a contribution towards breaching the wall of inhibitions that surrounds attitudes to politics in West Germany. Popular entertainment stars, for instance, in publicizing their political allegiances, promote a frank approach to politics and so help bridge the gap between the public and personal spheres, a bridge which is vital to the viability of liberal democracy, but which, for a variety of reasons, some of which have been touched on in this chapter, is not very strong in Germany.[11]

54

The 'student revolt' of recent years can also be seen against this background. It can be plausibly argued that the students – and in Germany the political mobilization of the students has not been restricted to an active and often extremist fringe, as in Britain – are the first post-war generation in Germany to have a healthy, normal, uninhibited attitude to politics. Previously, outspoken criticism of government risked being stamped as either Communist or Fascist inspired. The students at the end of the sixties seemed to have rid themselves of this complex. Admittedly their reaction against the lack of political involvement of previous years took the form of a fierce political engagement that for many people's taste was too dogmatic and intolerant. However, there is little doubt that they have forced public attention to focus on a number of problems that urgently required attention, and consequently brought about more participation in public political debate and the policy-making processes.

Illiberal Political Traditions

A number of leading German scholars have serious reservations about the long-term viability of West German liberal (or pluralistic) democracy. In one view, 'democracy is only acceptable to the Germans when it ensures a prosperous society which is at once unpolitical and anti-Communist, when the government establishes itself above the political parties and their despised horse-trading'.[12] In this view it was a mistake to assume that the apparent stability of the 'Adenauer era' was synonymous with the development of a stable parliamentary democracy in Germany. The fifties, at least where the growth of liberal democracy was concerned, was an abnormal interval, during which the Germans had been shielded from many of the hard facts of life. Reunification was linked with the 'economic miracle', with national prosperity, the Atlantic Alliance and European integration; it was going to 'happen' in their train. It was only with the building of the Berlin Wall in 1961 and with the appearance of cracks in the Western Alliance, that the realization began to dawn that time was not on the side of a tactic of postponement, of mere waiting, of trust in the automatic linking of Western integration and 'economic miracle' on the one hand, with reunification on the other. In foreign relations the sixties represented a 'normalization', a replacement of the apparent certainties of the fifties with the uncertainties and choices of the sixties. Domestically, too, the fifties had been abnormal; the exceptionally high growth rate had permitted the changing and competing demands of the pressure-groups, and the socio-economic groupings they represented, to be satisfied without the latent conflicts between them coming to a head. Again the sixties, at least most of the sixties, represented a 'normalization'. Prosperity remained, but growth rates fell, and as they fell conflicts emerged. This 'normalization' demanded alternative policies and brought with it the possibility of a change of governing party. Instead there was the *CDU/SPD* 'embrace' – a period during which the *SPD* remained formally in opposition but embraced most of the *CDU*'s policies ('the best *CDU* there ever was', *Die beste CDU, die es je gegeben hat,* was how one observer described the *SPD* during this period) – followed by the 'clinch' of the Grand Coalition (1966), with its hint of cartel and suggestion of flight from democratic political conflict. The 'normalization' of political conditions was followed by abnormality in the political system.

Other scholars point to the survival of German political traditions with strong illiberal connotations. In German political theory there has been a traditional confusion between the representative (or Anglo-Saxon) and the plebiscitary traditions of democracy, with their different theories of what constitutes the 'general will' of the people and of how best to arrive at the common good.[13] The distinction between the representative principle of the British parliamentary tradition (for which the 'general will' and the common good are not absolute values and do not infer a denial or inhibition of the political representation of individual and sectional interest),

56

and the plebiscitary principle (which postulates a pre-established 'general will', an identification of rulers and ruled, and assumes that the rule of the 'general will' necessarily leads to the realization of the common good), has been blurred in German democratic tradition, a confusion that was built into the Weimar Constitution and, to a much smaller extent, the Bonn Basic Law. The latter tradition, whose premiss is the 'nation one and indivisible', considers the promotion of sectional interest a threat to the substance of democracy. Not only the traditional contempt for the 'disruptive' and 'divisive' activities of political parties, but also the aversion to the activities of pressure-groups (which is a commonplace in Germany, whereas in most liberal democracies pressure-groups are now widely recognized as an essential prop on the democratic stage) derive in part from the difficulty which political theorists and practitioners, nurtured in the plebiscitary tradition, have in accepting that the socio-economic differentiations of modern industrial society must be accorded political relevance and allowed free expression in a liberal democracy. Perhaps the most outspoken and widely influential attack on West German democracy in recent years came from an exponent of this tradition, the philosopher, Karl Jaspers, whose book *Wohin treibt die Bundesrepublik?* became a best-seller. Political slogans such as Erhard's *formierte Gesellschaft* ('formed' or 'shaped' society) also fit into this background.

Another tradition of which it is authoritatively claimed that it has 'fashioned political thinking and practice in Germany up to today'[14] and which has illiberal implications, is the Hegelian concept of the 'neutral' state, 'above party', and 'acting in the interests of all'. Adherents of this tradition, without always making their premisses clear, attack liberal democracy from a platform of a monistic, as opposed to a pluralistic or liberal, view of the state. For them, political parties should get no further than the threshold of government; government itself should be a 'neutral' area, above party. Implicit in this view is a dichotomy of state and society, and a hostility towards the position political parties occupy in the foreground of politics in modern liberal democracies.

The Grand Coalition was also interpreted as an expression of what a leading German sociologist, Ralf Dahrendorf, terms the German 'longing for synthesis'.[15] According to him the Germans have an aversion to political and social conflict, including bodies like parliament which institutionalize conflict and 'wash dirty linen in public'. This aversion can lead to Utopian solutions of social conflict, of which the Nazi 'racial community' was the most extreme example. Adherents of this theory, who see examples of the 'aversion to conflict' in the principle of 'co-determination' for workers in German industrial relations and in the legal system, maintain that there is a tendency in German society to seek illusory 'once-and-for-all' solutions to conflicts instead of treating them as fruitful and potentially dynamic phenomena which require democratic *regulation* and *mediation*, but not a final solution. The recurrent exhortation of the Springer press to 'all pull together' is seen as another expression of this tendency. The 'aversion to conflict' is partly a reaction against the ideological, national and religious divisions which mark German history and is clearly linked to another recurring *motif*, the propensity for sacrificing *das Soziale* to *das Nationale*, for emphasizing national solidarity at the expense of the political expression of social diversity.

To interested foreigners, many of whom are impressed by the economic success of the Federal Republic and the apparent viability of the political system, the anxiety expressed by Bracher, Dahrendorf and others about German liberal democracy seems over-pessimistic, perhaps even a trifle overwrought. It should also be remembered that some of the criticisms just referred to, were made soon after the formation of the Grand Coalition. The decision of the *SPD* and the *FDP* to form a governing coalition in 1969, despite their very slender parliamentary majority and the suspect loyalty of a number of the *FDP* delegates, and the refusal of the *SPD* to be tempted into a continuation of the Grand Coalition, have put a different complexion on things, though the claim that underlying illiberal tendencies remain, is not invalidated.

The extent to which the contemporary division of Germany is bound to inhibit political debate and choice in West Germany (not to mention East Germany) should not be underestimated. In the present situation with Germany divided, opposition, in the shape of permanent, and usually unreasonable, criticism of West German policies, institutions and public figures, comes from the arch- (but German) enemy in the German Democratic Republic. The West German answer to this – though this has become less true in recent years – has often consisted in de-valuing domestic criticism and viewing with particular distrust any criticism which resembles that coming from the other side of the border. The fact that two hostile systems exist side by side on German soil tends to pervert all opposition into opposition between the systems and to deprive domestic conflicts of their political expression.

Viewed in this context it is scarcely surprising and perhaps understandable that for many Germans the 'black-red' Grand Coalition was a symbol – a symbol of the inner-German reconciliation, the end of the sorting into sheep and goats, Nazis and non-Nazis, exemplified by the co-operation in the same cabinet of Kiesinger (who was a member of the Nazi Party and held a senior position during the Third Reich), Brandt (Norwegian resistance against the Nazis) and Wehner (former Communist Party official who spent most of the Nazi period in exile).

References

[1] F. R. ALLEMANN, *Bonn ist nicht Weimar* (Köln, Kiepenhauer und Witsch, 1956).

[2] K. D. BRACHER, 'Ist Bonn doch Weimar?', in *Der Spiegel*, 13 March 1967.

[3] P. H. MERKL, *The Origin of the West German Republic* (New York, Oxford University Press, 1963), pp. 175, 176.

4 A. J. HEIDENHEIMER, *The Governments of Germany* (London, Methuen, 1965), pp. 74–6.

5 T. ESCHENBURG, *Die improvisierte Demokratie der Weimarer Republik* (Laupheim, Steiner, 1954).

6 G. LOEWENBERG, *Parliament in the German Political Process* (New York, 1966).

7 L. J. EDINGER, *Politics in Germany. Attitudes and Processes* (Boston, Little, Brown, 1968), pp. 105–22.

8 Ibid., pp. 84, 85.

9 R. B. TILFORD, and R. J. C. PREECE, *Federal Germany: Political and Social Order* (London, Oswald Wolff, 1969), pp. 67–79.

10 K. JASPERS, *The Future of Germany* (Chicago and London, University of Chicago Press, 1967).

11 R. DAHRENDORF, *Gesellschaft und Demokratie in Deutschland* (München, Piper, 1965), pp. 127–41.

12 K. D. BRACHER, in *Der Spiegel*, 13 March 1967.

13 E. FRAENKEL, 'Strukturdefekte der Demokratie und deren Überwindung', in E. Fraenkel and K. Sontheimer, *Zur Theorie der pluralistischen Demokratie* (Bonn, Bundeszentrale für Politische Bildung, 1964), pp. 8–16.

14 R. DAHRENDORF, op. cit., pp. 225–41.

15 Ibid., pp. 161–75.

3 The German Press

J. P. PAYNE

A Survey of Some of its Problems

Anyone from the West reading the 13 October 1969 copy of the East German newspaper *Neues Deutschland* would notice immediately that reporting in the East has quite a different flavour from that in the West. The paper bristles with optimism. The front-page headline proclaims: 'Sojus 7 launched. For the first time five cosmonauts in space.' Indeed this copy seems to be part of a serialized success-story telling of the Communist way of life: 'Foreign Guests in the German Democratic Republic – Friendly Meetings with Workers' (p. 2); 'Strength and Success of our Policy for Peace' (p. 5); 'Finishing Burst for This Year's Harvest' (p. 1). The journalist seems to feel one with the whole body of his readers and talks of '*our* Republic' and '*our* policy for peace' (my emphasis).

The picture the paper presents of the Western world is radically different: three people have been killed in street fighting in Belfast; workers are on strike in Italy and England; in West Germany a recent survey has shown that over 70 per cent of industry is owned by an *élite* of 305,000 families; and, to complete this picture of Western gloom, the British Conservative Party has ended its Brighton conference without agreeing on any definite programme.

There is no need to emphasize that this is manipulated reporting. *Neues Deutschland* is after all the organ of the *Zentralkommittee* of the East German Communist Party, the *Sozialistische Einheitspartei Deutschlands* (*SED*). Here the important events which have occurred in the course of the last twenty-four hours are reshaped to present a world which conforms to the most facile kind of Communist ideology: while 'Marxists' harvest in East Germany, 'Christians' kill each other in Belfast; while Soviet pioneers explore space, the 'USA aggressors' (p. 2) slaughter the Vietnamese.

The GDR journalist is expected, indeed instructed, to maintain this kind of bias. A central party directive in 1959 formulated the role of the journalist as follows: 'The socialist journalist thinks and acts as a party official, and puts heart and soul (*mit seiner ganzen Persönlichkeit dafür eintritt*) into the task of enlisting support for party and government decisions whether in his editorial work, in his public duties, in his community activities or in his personal life.'

The intention behind this directive is that the reporter should trace out in his reporting the social developments which the convinced Communist believe inevitable: the decline of Western capitalism and the rise of state socialism. The party directive, quoted above, insists that he should not fail to see the 'wood' (the Communist theory of social developments on a world scale) for the 'trees' (individual items of news). The same directive emphasizes that the Communist conviction is absolute and no other interpretation of world events is possible: 'the dilettante method of attaching a commentary to each item of news, instead of making the news a convincing commentary in itself, must be done away with.'

The whole of the directive, and this last statement in particular, run counter to the best traditions of reporting in the West where a clear distinction is made between information about events and the interpretation which is placed on them, i.e. between news and commentary. The objectivity of the coverage good newspapers offer is safeguarded by their being independent of the government of the country where they are produced and to a large extent free to print what their editors decide, without outside interference.

Of course, complete objectivity is nowhere a reality – it is not only in the GDR that the events of each day are distorted by other factors. The present article examines some of these distorting factors in the national press of the GFR but it should be emphasized that the situation in other Western countries, including Britain and the USA, also gives cause for concern.

Historical Perspectives

Before dealing with the present situation in the GFR one should take account of earlier developments in Germany. Between the wars nationalistic feeling, directed against the government and institutions of the Weimar Republic, ran very high. Alfred Hugenberg's communications empire which comprised many newspapers, a film company (which it is said he acquired because Eisenstein's film *The Battleship Potemkin* had had such a profound left-wing propaganda effect) and a news agency, conducted a continuous campaign against the Republic and against Marxism and Bolshevism. Hitler's rise to power was assisted by Hugenberg's propaganda which often had a more telling effect than views presented in the liberal and left-wing press and other media. (Hugenberg's own party, the *Deutschnationale Volkspartei* joined a national front with the National Socialists in October 1931.) From 1933 onwards, the media in Germany were gradually welded into a propaganda machine for the Nazi regime. The mildest reproof against the state or any party functionary led to imprisonment. In a speech in 1933 Goebbels, the Reich Minister for Propaganda, announced that the role of the press was to serve the government: 'Gentlemen, you will agree with me that the ideal would be a press so delicately organized that it becomes so to speak a piano on which the government can play, the ideal is where the press is an . . . instrument for swaying the masses, in the hands of the government.' It is ironic to see how closely this resembles the Communist view of the press as expounded in the 1959 directive quoted above. Both Fascist and Communist governments see the press not as a news medium, but as a propaganda weapon.

In 1945, on the collapse of the Third Reich, the Western

Allies saw that one of their most important tasks was to rebuild the press on a democratic basis; it was to be both independent and objective. Between 1945 and 1949 the Allies issued licences to publish newspapers to those people who had satisfactory records. The first paper to be licensed was the *Frankfurter Rundschau* whose licence-holders were three Social Democrats and four Communists – i.e. representatives of parties which had anti-Nazi records. Other German papers which have since gained an international reputation such as the *Frankfurter Allgemeine Zeitung* (*FAZ*) and *Die Welt*, and the weeklies *Die Zeit* and *Der Spiegel* were founded in this early post-war period. In 1949 when the Federal Republic came into existence, a licence to publish a newspaper was no longer required. The Basic Law (*Grundgesetz*), the provisional constitution for the GFR, guarantees the right of free expression of opinion and absence of censorship (Article 5, Paragraph 1). Those who drew up the *Grundgesetz* believed that the growth of democracy in the new republic depended on a vigorous and unhampered flow of information and comment between the government and the press which would be independent of each other, and on the individual's ability to derive information from a wide variety of sources and form his own considered opinion on issues of national and international concern. However other forces, not fully anticipated by the law-givers of 1949, have prevented their intentions from being fully realized.

Critical Views of Two Important West German Newspapers

The West German paper which enjoys perhaps the highest reputation abroad is the *Frankfurter Allgemeine Zeitung*. A careful examination of this paper was carried out by Hans Magnus Enzensberger who compared its reporting with that of the great newspapers of the world including *Le Monde*, *Neue Zürcher Zeitung*, *The Times* and *The New York Times*. It revealed disturbing omissions and flaws. There is not space to

give a full account of these nor of the subtlety and precision
of Enzensberger's approach. One or two examples must suffice.
He noted that the paper did not feature, as its main news item,
the events which almost all the other leading papers of the
world chose, although it is the stated intention of the paper to
select the most important news item in this way: 'From the
wealth of reports which flood in on the *FAZ* hour after hour
every day the editors seize the most important and most
interesting piece of news and make it the headline story.'
Enzensberger points out that, on 14 December 1961, the
editors of the *FAZ* were evidently of the opinion that the most
important and most interesting piece of world news was:
'Christmas Money – but only for Officials (*Beamte*) and Soldiers
on Active Service' – a headline which incidentally gives substance to another criticism that he levels against the paper: that
it concentrates too much on affairs which are of interest only to
German readers.

However a much more serious charge emerges from Enzensberger's examination of the reporting of talks in Paris in 1961
where Franz Josef Strauss, then Minister for Defence, brought
forward a plan for a NATO Nuclear Force with its own medium-
range rockets. He shows that the paper presented a distorted
view of what happened. It did not mention that Britain, the
USA and France were reluctant to consider the plan brought
forward by Strauss at that particular juncture since talks with
the Eastern Bloc were about to be held; Enzensberger disputes
several claims made by the paper, one of which was that
Strauss's 'concrete suggestions' had been accepted and that the
NATO council was broadly in agreement on the plan to develop
NATO as a nuclear force.

Enzensberger comes to the conclusion that the *FAZ* speaks a
special language prepared by the ruling classes for the lower
classes – he suggests that the news diet which is offered to the
latter is mixed to make the decisions of the former palatable.
The radical in Enzensberger is speaking here and one may be
sceptical of his aims, yet one is still disturbed by what he says:

65

that those who write the *FAZ*, though their work is not censored by any other authority, provide their own censorship. One senses, in reading the paper, that the editors feel that certain things may be said, but certain things may not be said. Let us leave this problem for a moment and pass to another paper.

Die Welt, another *überregional* paper of repute, can also be criticized for the inadequacies of its news presentation and its biased commentaries. The reader of the paper in the period after the Federal election in 1969 might have been forgiven for forgetting on occasion that the *CDU/CSU* were no longer in power. Even on the front page, the news section, reports on the activity of members of the new opposition predominate and the paper repeatedly interviews *CDU* opposition spokesmen on important issues. The leader page provides not the democratic concert of views, some left, some right of centre, that one might expect from a paper of this standing but a firm front against the policies of the *SPD/FDP* coalition government. Any kind of contact with the Eastern Bloc is viewed as weakness in the face of communism, any relaxing of defence efforts or criticism of NATO is cause for alarm. The paper campaigned against the Nuclear Non-Proliferation Treaty (commonly known in Germany as the *Atomsperrvertrag*), recently signed by the new government, seeing it as a threat to the defence of the West and a reduction of West German influence in the world. The advantages of the treaty were not given sufficient prominence. Here, as in the case of the *FAZ*, it is evident that either the editors have been selected for their adherence to a given political line or that some kind of pressure is being exerted to make them toe this line.

Problems within the West German Press

The left-wing radical (who has not been silent in Germany of late) has his answer ready when the problem of pressure is raised. He sees, or believes he sees, evidence of a plot by the rich to enslave the mass of the people by the intermediary of the consumer society which chains men to their place of work, the mass media which preach conformity to standards that support the *status quo*, and finally by the parliament which appears to be the voice of the people and is in fact the instrument of the rich. Even men of more moderate attitudes will see that this view, though exaggerated, can shed light on the workings of certain sectors of the press.

Those who drafted the Basic Law for the GFR failed to guarantee the freedom of the press except in the most general terms. In their anxiety to avoid the stigma of state interference they left this vital area of public life open to the inroads of big business (again one must emphasize that most other Western countries have succumbed to this problem as well).

The ranks of independent newspaper publishers in the Federal Republic have decreased steadily over the past years. From 1954 to 1964 the number of independent editorial staffs went down from 225 to 183. Today this has probably shrunk to around 150. Mergers and take-overs have been frequent. Firstly, to publish a newspaper one needs a large amount of capital for the printing machinery, and the 'raw material', newsprint itself, is expensive. In addition, the dynamic growth of the economy has increased the importance of advertising in the newspaper business; the average man has a good deal of money to spare and advertising in newspapers has expanded enormously to tempt him to spend it. Whereas before the war only about half the revenue of a given newspaper came from advertising, now it amounts to approximately two-thirds. (It is reported that a monthly subscription to *Die Welt*, which now costs DM 7·60, would cost DM 20 if no advertisements were carried.) But the advantage of having comparatively low-priced newspapers is more than outweighed by the disadvantages which advertising brings. A newspaper which for any reason starts to fall back in circulation will correspondingly start to be less attractive to an advertiser and advertising revenue will soon decrease; conversely, a paper with increasing sales will become increasingly more attractive to the advertiser. Over a period of time, therefore, the effect of advertising is to accelerate the growth or decline of a given publication. Unfortunately the newspapers with the largest circulation, which are correspondingly most attractive to advertisers, are not normally outstanding for the news and commentary they provide. Their success is based not on *informing* but on *pleasing* the public. The paper whose advertising fees are the highest (because it has by far the widest circulation of any paper in the Federal Republic), the *Bildzeitung*, is not, as we shall see, distinguished for the quality either of its information or its commentary. In 1959 its publisher, Axel Springer, made the following statement on what he thought most Germans were looking for in a newspaper: 'It has been obvious to me ever since the end of the war that there is one thing the German reader is most anxious to avoid and that is: having to think. My papers have been designed with this in mind.'

What has happened, as a distinguished sociologist, Ludwig von Friedeburg, has pointed out, is that the *Grundgesetz* has tended not so much to encourage among newspapers what he calls *Wettbewerb um Aufklärung*, i.e. competition to inform the reader about what is going on in Germany and the world, but rather that it has allowed economic competition (*wirtschaftlicher Wettbewerb*) between big press-concerns to grow unchecked. Since the Federal Government has not done anything to limit the power of the press groups, Axel Springer's publishing company, the largest in Germany, now has 70 per cent of the sales of daily newspapers in Berlin and Hamburg, 90 per cent of Sunday newspapers and 30 per cent of daily newspapers throughout the whole of the Federal Republic. In the field of the illustrated weekly magazines, five large concerns have the lion's share of the 50 million copies sold each week.

Economic concentration in the press becomes even less desirable when the publisher actually makes use of the political power placed in his hands and Springer is quite open about his political intentions. An advertisement in *The Times* by his group on 14 June 1969 listed these as follows: 'The Axel Springer publications stand for progress but oppose all attempts to destroy or subvert our society; support all peaceful moves to restore German unity in freedom; work for reconciliation between the Jewish and German people; reject any kind of political extremism; uphold the liberal market economy.' Newspapers in Springer's group take these policies as premises in their reporting and commentary, but their interpretation is often rather free. What are presented in many Springer papers as 'attempts to . . . subvert our society' – the theories and actions of certain students for example – are given serious consideration in other papers, notably *Die Zeit*, as a vital and healthy criticism of life in West Germany today. Springer newspapers tend to pursue a line of resistance to any attempt to start a serious dialogue with the Eastern Bloc, evidently because this is regarded as a form of 'political extremism' – when in fact it may be one of the first steps in negotiations which will lead ultimately to reunification. So, paradoxically, the rejection of 'extremism' might be a stumbling-block to the reunification of Germany.

Whatever the eventual effect of these policies, we find here a direct link between the opinions of a publisher and the views printed in papers distributed every day in their millions throughout the Federal Republic (at present about 8 million Springer newspapers are sold every day). Paul Sethe, a leading journalist, stated that the so-called 'freedom of the press' was really the freedom of the publishers: 'Press freedom is the freedom of two hundred rich people to spread their opinion.' And he continues: 'Journalists who share this opinion can always be found.'

The journalist in the centre of these interests must inevitably find his sphere of influence restricted. One journalist put his position cynically: *Wes Brot ich es', des Lied ich sing* – he knew which side his bread was buttered, realizing that his success in a given enterprise was linked to his ability to interpret the policies of his newspaper correctly and to adapt his articles accordingly. One wonders if the reporting of the *FAZ* on the world monetary crisis in May 1969, where the paper, quite uncharacteristically, campaigned for revaluation, was at all influenced by the fact that Karl Blessing, until recently the Director of the *Bundesbank*, who is Chairman of the body that administers the paper, had insisted on the need for a revaluation. (One must add, of course, that informed economic opinion throughout the country was for revaluation – however, even in the ranks of the *SPD*, despite the solidarity of *SPD* Economics Minister Schiller with Blessing, there was an anti-revaluation school of thought which deserved careful examination.) A more striking example of self-censorship is to be found in a statement by a reporter in a talk with some students in Munich about the Vietnam War. He said that he had not reported in his paper on the situation in South Vietnam, some time after 1954, when a majority had been in favour of union with North Vietnam since they felt that only the Communists were capable of maintaining an incorrupt administration. He explained his action (or rather inaction) as follows:

> First of all it was highly unlikely that my newspaper would have printed such a story. But in any case I would never have passed it on to my newspaper since, after all, we Germans owe the Americans a great deal and can't go stabbing them in the back. With every line I write I have to think of the journalist's heavy burden of responsibility, I have to think of the effect of what I write. And for these reasons I couldn't put down in writing what I have just told you.

This journalist here admits to two kinds of censorship: the censorship practised by his paper which is unwilling to print certain facts, and his personal censorship in interpreting his task as that of filtering out from his reports whatever he feels his readers ought not to know. I think that Enzensberger has demonstrated that both kinds of censorship were practised in the *FAZ*, at least in the early sixties; it is my belief that either kind of censorship is against the tenets of the *Grundgesetz* and usurps the right of the individual to form his own opinion. Such practices may be required by party officials in the East but should not be tolerated in the West.

There is no lack of critics of the press in West Germany. Herbert Wehner, a prominent *SPD* politician, voiced his criticisms in the strongest possible form: 'We have a press which is simply too bad to be true (*eine Presse, die unter aller Kritik ist*). It doesn't inform, its reporting is prejudiced (*sie schreibt auf Grund von vorgefassten Meinungen*).' Axel Springer, in particular, has been attacked by many prominent West German personalities. Ralf Dahrendorf, a leading sociologist and *FDP* member of parliament, has urged Springer not to try to influence political opinion. Günter Grass, possibly the best-known author in West Germany at the moment and an active critic of West German life, has accused Axel Springer of being a threat to parliamentary democracy and using 'fascist methods'. Golo Mann, the son of Thomas Mann and a leading historian states: 'The concentration of power in Springer's hands has become a central problem in the Federal Republic.' Despite the barrage of criticism very little has been done.

The German Press Council (*Der Deutsche Presserat*), a body of publishers and journalists formed in 1956, has confined its attentions to comparatively minor problems. Commissions have been set up but have had little effect. The *Michel-Kommission* investigated competition between the publicly owned radio and television networks and private publishing concerns. The *Günther-Kommission* which investigated the press itself could hardly be considered an independent body since it included Springer and several other publishers. The Commission's report submitted in 1968 does suggest that the present situation in the press is 'endangered' (*gefährdet*) but even if its proposals were implemented by the government – which is unlikely in the foreseeable future – the present concentrations would be left intact. It is doubtful whether Axel Springer's decision to sell some of the glossy magazines he owned (among them *Das Neue Blatt*, *Eltern* and *Jasmin*) was strongly influenced by the Commission's findings. It seems more probable, even to the

Commission's chairman, that this was a political move to strengthen his drive for the introduction of commercial television (known as *Verlegerfernsehen*) in which he wants to be represented.

Criticism of the press has, however, constantly had to reckon with the fear among Germans, understandable in view of their experiences during the Third Reich, that any intervention by the government in the press, might pave the way for state manipulation of news and commentary. To this well-founded fear must be added another: the politicians' concern that the anger of the press might be directed against them or their party. (Helmut Schmidt, at present the Minister for Defence, has said that anyone who attacks Springer is committing political suicide and when an *SPD* student publication attacked Springer in an election year, leading politicians, among them Herbert Wehner and Willy Brandt, bent over backwards to dissociate themselves and their party from the 'incriminating' article.)

Two of Springer's Publications
1 *Die Welt*

In the brief survey of the line adopted by *Die Welt* it was quite clear that its reporting was one-sided. This present situation stands in stark contrast to what the British authorities hoped for shortly after the war when they established the paper in their occupation zone. They had in mind something similar to *The Times*. Capital for the undertaking was requisitioned by the British authorities and in 1949 the stock was transferred to six trustees, five German and one English. The paper got into financial difficulties and in the early 1950s it was necessary to sell. What then happened can be seen to some extent as typical of the development of the West German press.

The paper was first offered to the *Deutsche Gewerkschaftsbund* (*DGB* – very approximately the equivalent of the British 'Trades Union Congress') but they hesitated to take it over; the idea of making it into a public corporation like the radio stations was

72

considered – the *SPD* press officer, Heine, negotiated with a *CDU* member of parliament, Bucerius (Bucerius is the publisher of *Der Stern* and *Die Zeit* and it is interesting that his merger with the firm Gruner & Jahr was forced on him by competition from Axel Springer), but it is reported that before they could reach any decision on this proposal their talks were cut short by the British representative. Several private groups were interested in acquiring *Die Welt*, among them the Ullstein Verlag which was just starting up its activities again in Berlin.

It was then that Springer (who, even at this early stage, was a force to be reckoned with, owing to the success of his first ventures which included *Hör zu*, a radio programme periodical and, among other newspapers, *Bildzeitung*, which was beginning to make its mark) began negotiations with *Welt–Verlagsleiter* Heinrich Schulte. It had been decided that the company to be formed was to be a *Stiftung* – an autonomous organization run by the employees rather than a board of directors. During negotiations with Schulte the idea that 10 per cent of the share capital should be assigned to the employees was dropped. Instead, 5 per cent was to go to the *Stiftung* and 5 per cent to the purchaser, Springer; on 8 May 1953, while these negotiations were going on, the *Hamburger Echo* – an *SPD* paper which like so many of the party newspapers since the war did not prove competitive and eventually ceased publication in 1966 – warned of the dangers of a power concentration if Springer's bid for *Die Welt* went through. But in mid-May the sale to Springer was agreed to – he acquired a 75 per cent interest in the paper for what seems to have been a very low price. A rival group, the Broschek concern immediately matched Springer's offer but was informed that the sale was already complete.

It has been noted that after such a long waiting period – the paper had been up for sale for a year – the final transfer was completed in a remarkably short space of time. Two events may help to explain this. The first was a meeting between Konrad Adenauer and Axel Springer in April 1953 at the *CDU* party conference in Hamburg, the second was Adenauer's visit to

London from 14 to 16 May, where the Federal Chancellor urged the sale of the paper to Springer (as we saw above, one of the trustees was English). Whether there was any kind of agreement between Springer and Adenauer may never be known, but it is certain that the Springer press threw the weight of its support behind the *CDU/CSU* leaders and has helped to make their policies acceptable to the public. Hans Zehrer, an old friend of Springer's, took over as editor-in-chief of *Die Welt*. This was a strange twist of fate because he had originally been selected for the post of editor of this paper by the British authorities shortly after the war but had been dismissed before the paper started to appear; the reason for this was a chorus of protests from the *SPD*-dominated city authorities who had not forgotten that before the war Hans Zehrer had attacked liberalism and marxism in newspaper articles (Adenauer's judgement of the new editor-in-chief was expressed in one word: *Wirrkopf!*). Through friendship with members of the *Welt-Stiftung* (whose inner organization is kept secret) and of course through the intermediary of his 75 per cent interest in the concern, Springer was assured of a decisive interest in the paper, in spite of its officially independent status.

After a visit to Moscow in 1958, Springer's ideas hardened. *The Times* gives a brief pen-picture of Springer: 'Even in bed at night he fiercely snips his papers and scribbles notes to his editors that are carefully culled from the floor each morning by an aide.' There is quite clearly a difference between the publishers like Lord Thomson whose obsession with the business-side of his undertaking is legendary (on a visit to Moscow he offered to buy both *Pravda* and *Isvestia*!), and who, apart from his active support for a free enterprise economy, expresses little interest in politics as such, and Springer who though an acute businessman sees himself primarily as a man with a mission to reunite Germany. 'I'll reunite Germany, whether you believe it or not', he told one of his editors who had expressed doubts about chances for reunification; on another occasion he is reported to have written: 'I must break with (Paul) Sethe – he'll

74

spoil my efforts for reunification.' The sense of a personal duty to bring about reunification, which Springer expresses here, is disquieting in a man who has so much power in his hands – one can also understand why, for all the solemn renunciations of force reiterated by West German politicians, some central European countries find it difficult to suppress their fears of West German nationalism. There is evidently some connection between Springer's views and the fact that since 1960 many well-known journalists and foreign correspondents have left *Die Welt*. The newspaper has undoubtedly suffered from this exodus.

2 *Bildzeitung*

The newspaper with the largest sales in Germany is *Bildzeitung* (known simply as *Bild*), owned as we have seen by Springer. Estimates of its daily circulation vary between 4 and 5 million copies; it is certainly read by at least 10 million Germans every day. Though a far cry from a quality newspaper, sheer turnover gives the paper deep political significance. The average person cannot get to his place of work without being tempted several times to buy a copy, for *Bild* is sold on street corners, in station bookshops, kiosks and small shops. The price is low for a paper: 20 pfennigs, compared with 50 pfennigs per copy for *FAZ*. Even if the individual does not buy a copy, he will probably have read the headline at least once (possibly while sitting opposite someone in a bus). In short this newspaper is undoubtedly a fact in the consciousness of most West Germans, in the same way as a television commercial, however banal, will creep into the minds of the most serious people. Though the paper offers a very limited range of news and is pitched to appeal to those with a limited education, it is read by people from all walks of life. Adenauer could occasionally be seen looking through a copy of *Bild* in the *Bundestag*. He realized that it was through the pages of the paper that the mass of Germans found out what the government was doing and that this paper influenced the public's feelings towards the government to a significant extent. (It is perhaps worth noting that the serious newspaper which Adenauer read was not German at all, but Swiss – the *Neue Zürcher Zeitung*!)

Haseloff, a psychologist who took part in a recent seminar on the German press, noted that the average reader wants a wide range of information from the newspaper but that he also wants the newspaper itself to perform the task of relating the information to his own existence. But the average reader also demands, paradoxically enough, something which Haseloff describes as *Entlastung von einem Realitätsdruck*. By this he understands the inclusion in the paper of articles that direct the reader's attention *away from* the serious issues of the day. *Bild* fulfils these demands to a large extent. It covers a wide range of 'human interest' stories: the cat rescued from a tree; the lorry-driver driving off from an East German customs' check who hears shots ring out from the back of his lorry, where a customs guard is still conducting a search, etc. It provides relief from the humdrum with reports of sex and crime. But let us examine, in the following paragraphs, how political reports in *Bild* are 'made relevant' to the life of its readers.

Although none of the complexities of a given event can be analysed in the very limited space available in *Bild* for this kind of coverage, the reporting of major political events does give a certain air of finality, as if all that needed to be said is expressed succinctly in *Bild*. In reading the paper, the reader, though still uninformed, is encouraged to feel that he is in possession of the major facts of the issues of the day. The editors' views on these issues emerge clearly in the act of reporting. There is no clear differentiation between information and commentary. Thus the paper appears to present to the reader the 'reality of the day' reduced to its essentials and in the presentation the 'proper reaction' to this 'reality' is suggested. The paper helped to pave the way for the formation of the Grand Coalition in 1966 by playing down the alternatives to the Coalition and insisting on the suitability of Kurt Georg

Kiesinger for the office of Chancellor, despite his very limited experience of federal politics.

However, any examination of the paper's political stance reveals a number of paradoxes. As we have seen Springer pledged the support of his group for the cause of reunification; but the support which *Bild* gave to the government during the vital formative years of the Federal Republic may have done the cause of reunification some damage. (This is of course controversial. On Adenauer's list of priorities reunification came *after* the security of the new state and its integration into the West. This led him to make no answer to a plan for reunification put forward by the East in 1952. It is by no means certain that this offer was genuine but it could at least have been explored. See the article by R. Cecil in this book.) The paper is designed to appeal, we have seen, to the large majority of the people of West Germany and purports to represent their interests; consistently, however, the paper has pursued policies which have favoured businessmen. When metal-workers went on strike in 1963 the paper cried national disaster: *Wirtschaftswunder am Ende* ('The End of the Economic Miracle'); and in 1969 during the May monetary crisis the paper would have nothing to do with the idea of revaluation (though, as we have seen, this was recommended by experts, and failure to revalue in fact led to a certain amount of inflation in Germany which hit the average German quite hard). It told the politicians, in no uncertain terms, to 'get their hands off' the mark. Here the *Bild* was actually confusing its readers, who probably knew little enough about economics anyway, by appealing to the very real fear in the minds of the Germans that once again their currency would lose almost all its value. (The words 'revaluation' (*Aufwertung*) and 'devaluation' (*Abwertung*) mean the same thing for many Germans!) Whether the issue is strike or revaluation, one senses that the paper does not have the interests of the mass of people at heart. But possibly the most serious paradox which reporting in the paper presents is that, though committed to uphold democracy in West Germany, it appears to have in fact encouraged a re-emergence of authoritarian thinking. In 1967 *Bild* and other newspapers reported that a bomb attack on Vice-President Humphrey had been planned by students but was, by good fortune, averted by the police. This was gross misrepresentation of the facts – a demonstration had certainly been planned but the 'bombs' were filled with flour. In this way *Bild* and other newspapers have tended to give large sections of the student population a bad name and in so doing have done much to gloss over the serious and substantial criticisms made by students of the present state of democracy in West Germany. One wonders how far the attacks by citizens of German cities on long-haired youth is prompted by a true understanding of left-wing ideology and intentions, and how far by *Bild*.

Two Non-Springer Publications: *Die Zeit* and *Der Spiegel*

Springer asserts that, as long as one concern does not control all the newspapers in West Germany, the freedom of the press is assured. Few would agree with him. However, one must emphasize that there remain in Germany many newspapers and periodicals which pursue an independent line, attempt to report objectively on the news and offer the reader carefully considered opinions of national and international developments. I shall examine briefly two of the best known of these.

Die Zeit, a weekly newspaper with a circulation of over 200,000, has an outstanding editorial staff and supplements their articles with contributions by politicians, professors and other experts – mainly, but by no means exclusively, from Germany – on issues of national and international concern. Though liberal in outlook, it occasionally throws its columns open to more radical thinking. It has helped to make the public more conscious of short-comings in the life of the Federal Republic. Recently the following have been critically examined: the question of how far democracy is alive in Germany at the moment, the situation in the German universities, and American industrial influence in Europe. Proof of the refusal of the editors to bow to the interests of big business is found in several frank accounts of the life of the factory-worker – the striking title of one disturbing article, dealing with the mental stress which accompanies production-line work, bears this out: 'Worn out in the work process, Hans B., thirty-one years old, can't sleep.'

Contrasting with, yet complementing, *Die Zeit* is the left-wing weekly news magazine, *Der Spiegel*, which has a format similar to the American magazines *Time* and *Newsweek* but which is otherwise quite different from them. Its main field of interest is politics and its reporting of current political issues is supplemented by conversations between *Spiegel* reporters and prominent men – the well-known *Spiegel-Gespräche*. Where *Bild* tends to cloud political issues, *Der Spiegel* tries to penetrate the corridors of power and in so doing presents politicians as fallible human beings. Politicians are nervous of being portrayed in *Der Spiegel* since this magazine often formulates its views in polemical fashion. Essentially this is a virtue – *Der Spiegel* has gained a reputation unparalleled in the *Bundesrepublik* for its outspoken commentary on political and social problems – but sometimes it oversteps the mark. A recent attack on Eugen Gerstenmaier, formerly President of the *Bundestag*, amounted to caricature and character assassination. On occasions performing the 'spy for democracy' role has got the magazine into hot water. The best-known case was in 1962 when Franz Josef Strauss, then Minister of Defence ordered the seizure of the *Spiegel* building and the imprisonment of its leading editors including the publisher Rudolf Augstein, on a charge of high treason for having betrayed vital defence secrets. (See also the article by R. B. Tilford.) This in fact did the magazine little harm and indeed gave it overnight an international reputation. The critical stance is present even in some of the photographs reproduced in *Der Spiegel*. One of these, taken at a rally of the extreme right-wing party, the *NPD*, is entitled *NPD-Ordner*. The picture is dominated by the huge stomach of one of the steel-helmeted *NPD* anti-heckler squad. Another, a front-page

79

photograph, shows the former *CDU* Chancellor Kiesinger, full face, caught in a cover-girl pose with one hand framing a cheek.

The paper has become an institution in the Federal Republic, with close to a million readers (who, according to a recent survey by the magazine, spend an astonishing weekly average of four hours and five minutes reading its pages!). Many of these readers collect the magazines using them as a kind of contemporary history series and reference work. The paper has a huge archive dealing with contemporary history, the *Spiegel-Archiv*, whose staff checks the information contained in articles before publication. The success of the periodical has swollen its length to 250 pages or more, much of which is taken up with advertisements – a necessary concession to the trends of the time, as was the recent decision to have the magazine printed on Springer presses. (In view of the frequent attacks on Springer which have been published in the magazine, this last move must have required some heart-searching on Augstein's part.) Even Enzensberger, after exposing several of the weaknesses of *Der Spiegel*, was forced to admit that the magazine was indispensable.

It would be wrong to conclude this survey of the problems and weaknesses of the press in the GFR without mentioning the essential role of the provincial press at which other countries cast many a look of envy. Even in this age which is dominated by big business, the provincial press has continued to thrive in Germany and has resisted absorption into large concerns.

Postscript (May 1970)

Since this article was written there has been a significant development on the German press scene. Axel Springer has sold one-third of his concern to the Bertelsmann publishing group.

It may seem that this move goes some way to turning the thrust of attacks on Springer's position of influence – and, to judge by what he has said on the subject, Springer hopes and expects that this will be the case. There is no doubt that the barrage of criticism to which Springer has been subjected has contributed to his change of policy. (It is argued that, with the new government, Springer feared possible legislation against his position of power and simply decided to sell while he still had room for manoeuvre.) However the critics refuse to be shaken off so lightly. Although Springer has sold the shares in question they remain in his trusteeship until 1972, the Bertelsmann group having left decision-making entirely in his hands until that date. This effectively leaves the present situation untouched until 1972. Even after 1972, Springer may be in a position to maintain his influence in the company which bears his name although some of the shares of the company will have passed out of his control. He has seen to it that the tenets of his publisher's philosophy (as listed earlier) are established in the statutes of the newly formed Axel Springer stock company.

Setting these doubts aside we are confronted with more serious eventualities. Technology now offers man the opportunity to revolutionize the communications industry. Let us take, as an example, the book trade. Here, in the present system, a large number of books is printed in a given edition and then distributed over a wide area to various book-shops where they await the purchaser – a process which involves the costs of paper, printing, transportation and storage without the guarantee of returns which will provide a profit or even cover costs. In the future, data representing the layout of the pages, the illustrations and type, etc. of a given publication may be stored in a central computer which, on receipt of a given number of orders for the text in question, can supply the necessary instructions to a printing plant (possibly one in another city) which will print the exact number of books ordered. This system can be applied to periodicals, dictionaries, etc., as well as to books.

A further idea, which given the necessary capital can readily be realized, is the storage of articles and papers from important journals, dealing with the most recent advances in scientific research, in a computer which can then supply an expert in any given field with the up-to-date information he requires. Indeed the time seems not far off when, as events take place throughout the world, they will be recorded in computers from which information is channelled to newspapers, radio and television stations and also stored in preparation for inclusion in books, films or documentaries on contemporary issues.

The business world has realized the opportunities which this technological potential offers. Groups of firms are already working towards a situation which has been described as 'integrated multi-media publishing' in which all kinds of printed matter (not only books, newspapers, periodicals, etc., but also material for radio and television programmes and films) can be produced from a central fund of information stored in a single computer complex.

The Bertelsmann group embraces more than fifty firms, including the largest book-club in the world, the largest book printing plant (100,000 books a day!) and the largest film distributing service. It possesses an electronic indexing system which supplies clients with lists of addresses for advertising promotions, marketing surveys and other purposes. With its development of data retrieval systems the Bertelsmann group is attempting to make the technological possibilities now available work to its own business advantage. In addition to the publishing houses it owns, it possessed last year most of the technical capacity required to establish an information network of the kind envisaged above. In 1969 a further step was taken. The Bertelsmann group added a quarter share in the firm of Gruner & Jahr, which as we saw earlier, publishes a number of leading periodicals. With the $33\frac{1}{3}$ per cent participation in Axel Springer's group it acquired in 1970, it is calculated that Bertelsmann now has an interest in 24 per cent of newspapers in the Federal Republic and 35 per cent of the periodicals. It is true that as yet this is not a controlling interest but there is no legal barrier at the moment to Bertelsmann acquiring control where it now merely participates. The power placed in the hands of those who direct such a group would be immeasurable. The present diversification of sources of information (broadcasting services, newspapers, books, etc.) might overnight, as it were, become merely different outlets for information whose source, the computer 'bank', was controlled by the management of one or two mammoth groups in a given country.

This is a problem which the new West German government will have to look into very carefully.

Select Bibliography

GÜNTER BÖDDEKER, *20 Millionen täglich* (Oldenburg and Hamburg, Gerhard Stalling Verlag, 1967).

HANS MAGNUS ENZENSBERGER, *Einzelheiten I: Bewusstseins - Industrie* (Frankfurt am Main, Suhrkamp Verlag, 1962).

E. M. HERMANN, *Zur Theorie und Praxis der Presse in der Sowjetischen Besatzungszone Deutschlands* (Berlin, Colloquium Verlag, 1963).

HANS DIETER JAENE, *Der Spiegel - Ein deutsches Nachrichten - Magazin* (Frankfurt am Main, Fischer Bücherei G.m.b.H., 1968).

BERND JANSEN and ARNO KLÖNNE (eds.), *Imperium Springer* (Köln, Pahl-Rugenstein Verlag, 1968).

HERMANN MEYN, *Massenmedien in der Bundesrepublik Deutschland* (Berlin, Colloquium Verlag, 1968).

HANS DIETER MÜLLER, *Der Springer-Konzern* (München, R. Piper & Co., 1968).

BERGEDORFER PROTOKOLLE, *Bedroht die Pressekonzentration die freie Meinungsbildung?* (Hamburg, R. N. Decker's Verlag, 1967), Band 19.

HANS SCHUSTER and LEO SILLNER, *Die Zeitung* (München, Günter Olzog Verlag, 1968).

4 The Structure of German Society after the Second World War[1]

J. FIJALKOWSKI

The GFR is today one of the most powerful industrial nations in the world and its political life seems more stable than that of other West European nations. The problems of the early post-war years seem to have vanished with the heaps of rubble after the defeat of Nazi Germany. Those who drew up the Basic Law intended to make the GFR a constitutional democracy with a fair social order (*rechtstaatliche und soziale Demokratie*) and to-day's politicians make out that this is just what has happened. But this view is in fact disputed from different quarters. On the one hand the GDR which occupies a position in the camp of East European Socialist states, similar to that of the GFR in the Western Bloc, claims to be a bulwark of true democracy against the powerful growth of West German capitalism and expansionism. On the other hand, within the GFR itself, radical-democrats consider that the country has seen a restoration of a society with privileged classes where 'democracy' is only a veneer. The GFR, so they argue, is far from being a constitutional, social democracy. In the following pages we shall bear these differences of opinion in mind while we examine the development of West German society since the end of the Second World War.

The Situation at the End of the War

Many of the post-1949 developments were already implicit in what happened immediately after the war. The National

[1] I am indebted to H. Schmollinger for his suggestions and assistance in preparing this article.

84

Socialist Germany which plunged Europe into war was a society that had emerged from the breakdown of earlier experiments in liberal democracy within an essentially conservative tradition. This state which attempted to channel internal crises into imperialist aggression was utterly destroyed. When the victorious allies analysed the origins of fascism they came to different conclusions and evolved different occupation policies. The Soviets were of the opinion that fascism could only be stamped out, and a democratic Germany could only be created, if the traditional structures of bourgeois society were abolished; the Western Allies thought that it would be enough to break up the large business concerns and carry out a 'denazification' of public life to direct the country towards constitutional democracy. But with the Cold War, the powers which had been allied in war against a common enemy became aware that their social orders were incompatible and their political interests irreconcilable. It became increasingly difficult to reach agreement on policy towards Germany. The German people themselves, drained of all concern for politics in the day-to-day struggle for physical survival, were blind to the situation they were confronted with as a nation and were incapable of planning for the future. It is remarkable, however, that wherever the voice of the people was heard, there was a definite demand for the extension of public control and ownership of the economy (*Sozialisierung*). This tender plant of anti-fascism which had sprung from German soil was, however, not allowed to grow in freedom. The reparations policies of the British and French occupation forces restricted its growth, and the radical restructuring of society by the Soviet forces which left no room for constitutional democracy, trampled it underfoot. With the start of the American programme for European reconstruction, which was rejected on ideological grounds by the Soviet zone and which led to the setting up of the Bizone in West Germany (the Bizone was an economic link-up of the American and British occupation zones in 1947), the spontaneous demand in Germany for *Sozialisierung* was stifled. The USA which financed the European Recovery

85

Programme (ERP) excluded such a policy. Social and political differences between America and Russia became more pronounced and this led ultimately to the division of Europe where the Soviet occupation zone of Germany on the one hand, and the three Western occupation zones on the other, were absorbed into two different international systems: the result was two separate states in Germany. The German currency reform of 1948 was, in retrospect, one of the most important turning-points. It was undertaken in Germany with a view to participation in the ERP. It favoured those who owned property and other real goods and penalized those who had only paper money or bank accounts. At the same time a sharing-out of wealth, an equalization of burdens (*Lastenausgleich*) between those who still owned goods, land and stocks, etc., and those who had lost all their possessions, was instituted. A generous system of social security was promised as well. The currency reform in the West led to a recovery which quickly outpaced the Soviet zone. But at the same time it started a development which, though it brought undoubted economic success, failed to implement many desirable social policies. Fear of the political repression that characterizes life in the other part of Germany turned the attention of West Germans away from conditions at home. For even the equalization of burdens and the system of social security did not prevent the gradual restoration of capitalism in West Germany, once the decision not to follow a policy of *Sozialisierung* had been taken. It is now very difficult to realize the original intentions of creating a constitutional, social democracy. Since the future is in the hands of the younger generations it is important, in any close analysis of problems and tendencies in German society, to look briefly at the way generation 'change-over' and civic culture are related.

Civic Culture and Generation 'Change-over' (*Generationsverschiebungen*)

Social structures and the political framework of a country affect what people do and what they do not do. They rest on attitudes

86

of mind which do vary but which are fundamentally a product of these same structures. Structural change can only come about through changed attitudes and this only happens over a considerable period of time. Historical experiences may act as a political catalyst for change in the social order but only when a new generation with new attitudes takes over from an earlier generation. To understand developments in the GFR over the last twenty years, it is useful to examine the generation change-overs which have taken place.

Statistics show that the population of West Germany bears the scars of recent history. Of those alive now in the GFR, a disproportionately small percentage was born towards the end of the First World War and right after the Second World War and at the time of the Depression around 1930. The percentage of old people who are no longer capable of supporting themselves is rising with the rise in the life-expectancy and will continue to do so until 1985. The number of soldiers killed in the war is reflected in several year groups where women form a large majority. This is particularly evident in the case of the older generation. It is even more interesting to compare the age composition of the population in 1950 and 1967. This makes the changes which have taken place in the civic culture very clear.

Table 1   *Composition of the population according to the year of birth* (expressed as a percentage of the population)

Year of birth between	1950	1967
1850–80	5·6	0·3
1880–1905	27·8	15·8
1905–30	35·7	30·2
1930–50	30·9	28·0
1950–67	0·0	25·7

Calculated according to *Statistisches Jahrbuch* (1952), p. 25; (1969), p. 34.

At the time when the GFR came into existence over two-thirds of the population had been born before 1930. Indeed a third of the population had been born before 1905, having spent their formative childhood years in the Wilhelmine age of authoritarianism. For the larger part of their adult existence they had known particularly difficult times: the First World War, the troubled years of the Weimar Republic, the Nazi seizure of power and the Second World War that followed soon after. They bear collective responsibility, whatever their individual role, for this segment of history. At the end of the Second World War they were long past their prime.

Those born between 1905 and 1930 had lived through the collapse of the Weimar Republic and the Nazi seizure of power and provided a reservoir for soldiers to fight in the front lines. When the GFR was founded they were aged between twenty and forty-five. If one takes the denazification procedures of the Allies as one's yardstick, they were also required to accept responsibility for Germany's descent into National Socialism and imperialist war. To this generation, as much as to the generation of those born before 1905, the newly emerging states, the GFR and the GDR, were entrusted. The remainder of the population (about one-third of the total) consisted of children and young people under twenty years of age.

In the meantime a significant change has taken place in the composition of the GFR according to age-groups. Those born before 1905 now make up only 16 per cent of the population. The generation of those born between 1905 and 1930 now represents somewhat less than one-third of the population, and these people – now aged between thirty-five and sixty-five and, accordingly, to a large extent beyond the prime of life – form the 'establishment' of the GFR. This generation has come under increasing pressure from the younger generation: those born after 1930 now make up well over half the population. These younger people cannot be held responsible for the failure of the Weimar Republic, the rise of Nazism and the Second World War, although many of them received part of their education in the Nazi period. The most remarkable thing about the present age-grouping in West Germany is that more than a quarter of the population was born after 1950. It was only after the founding of the GFR that most of the parents of these young people reached the age of maturity and they view the time between the wars as past history. Their children are totally unaware of the tensions of the Cold War which overshadowed the first years of the GFR, whereas the division of Germany and the affluent society are familiar features of the world they live in, as is freedom of travel throughout western Europe.

This enormous shift in the composition of the population of West Germany helps to explain the changes in the attitude towards, and evaluation of, contemporary Germany and the world at large. Herein lies the hope for a more complete realization of constitutional, social democracy in Germany.

The Problem of the Expellees and Refugees

One of the earliest and most serious problems of West German society was the integration of the expellees and refugees (i.e. Germans from parts of Germany which had been appropriated by other powers or from non-German countries where they or their ancestors had settled, who after the war were forced to go to those parts of Germany which are now the GFR and the GDR). Up till 1949, 7·6 million of these Germans had come to what is now the GFR from the territories east of the Oder-Neisse boundary (the Eastern border of the present GFR); in addition 1·4 million refugees had arrived from what was then the Soviet occupation zone. Up till 1961, the year when the Berlin Wall was built and the GDR was hermetically sealed off from the GFR, the number of refugees from the GDR rose to over 3 million and the number of those who had left areas which are now part of Poland rose to about 9 million. In 1961 about half the total of refugees from the GDR were young people. Refugees and expellees, together with their children, many of them born in the GFR, today make up about one-fifth of the total population. This influx of refugees caused several problems. The immediate effect was to make supplies more scarce.

There was also a potential political problem in that the refugees might develop a party which would be a hotbed of resentment and a breeding-ground for ideas of revenge. An organization, the *Block der Heimatvertriebenen und Entrechteten* (*BHE*: 'League of those who have been driven from their homeland and divested of their rights') tried to forge the interests of these people into a political weapon. But the expanding economy, the attempts of all other political parties to solicit the votes of the *BHE* and the success in integrating the refugees (a special ministry was set up for this purpose), all helped to overcome this danger. Under the twenty years of *CDU* government the feelings of resentment were channelled into a loyalty towards the GFR but also into acceptance of conservative policies. The refugees' eagerness to work hard and make a home for themselves provided a boost to the economy and also meant that feelings of resentment could not take root, with the result that now the *BHE* has left the political arena altogether. Indeed the integration of refugees was organized so successfully that, together with the economic boom, it encouraged more and more people to flee the GDR. The extent to which the refugees have become citizens of the GFR is most evident when one considers that the coalition of *SPD* and *FDP* which came to power in 1969 could afford, among other things, to move towards recognition of the Eastern borders of the GDR (which would mean that the home of many Germans, land which had belonged to Germany for centuries, would be recognized by a German government to be foreign soil). Fewer and fewer refugees express the desire to return to their homes in the East and this tendency is being accelerated by the younger generation who consider the GFR to be their home.

Problems of Settlement and Housing

The influx of refugees made the housing shortage in West Germany more acute. In 1950 more than half of the population was living in subtenants' lodgings or barracks. In more recent years the problem has eased and only one-tenth of the population now lives in such accommodation. Of the 18·5 million dwellings, some 20 per cent are owner-occupied. However other problems have taken the place of the earlier shortage.

Rents have risen so sharply that it is becoming difficult for old-age pensioners and families with many children to find somewhere to live. This development has followed the premature ending of central control of housing. Private initiative in house-building has been encouraged, the construction of dwellings being viewed primarily as a source of profit rather than as the provision of a suitable home environment. This has led to the all-too-common sight in West Germany of row upon row of one- and two-family houses – a deplorable waste of valuable building land – profitable for the owner but not very pleasant for the tenant.

The policy of encouraging private building, favouring those with quite high incomes, was founded both on the idea 'to each his own home' and on the desire to extend private ownership in the economy. Once, however, a person has decided to build his own home, the undertaking consumes all his energy and earnings. The high cost of house construction, which leads to decades of debt for the owner, together with the poor quality of building, means that at the point where the debts are paid off and he is supposed to sit back and enjoy his home, the property is usually in need of considerable repair. In this way the house-owner is constantly forced to mobilize his income in the upkeep of his home and is usually unable either to improve his education, or to take any kind of action at work which, though in the long run it might result in a radical improvement in conditions there, might also interrupt the flow of money he needs. In short, though the ownership of one's own home is prestigious, it restricts personal and social freedom.

The population-drift from the country into the large towns and cities has made housing problems more acute. Dormitory suburbs have sprung up after the pattern mentioned above. They tend to be some distance away from the city centre and from the factories and businesses where those who live in them work. Indeed many of the hours gained by a shorter working week are often lost in heavy traffic on the way to work.

The situation has reached such a pass that one must ask whether the GFR can still lay claim to being a socially just society while private speculation is allowed such free rein in the field of housing.

Only recently have attempts been made to plan industrial complexes, housing developments and cultural facilities in some sort of meaningful relationship to each other. This positive development has however met with the entrenched resistance of local government (*kommunale Selbstverwaltung*) which (after the war) the Western Allies, but not the Russians, had tried to strengthen as part of their policy of creating a decentralized administration in Germany. Here we have a definite conflict of interest between planning efficiency, requiring a strong central authority, and the democratic demand that the elected representatives of, for example, a small town, should have a say in the planning of their environment.

Social Developments Reflected in a Survey of Occupations and Earnings

It will help us to decide whether the GFR has seen a restoration of a society with privileged and underprivileged classes or has in fact developed towards constitutional, social democracy, if we examine firstly, the way the numbers of people in certain social status groups have increased or decreased (see Table 2), and secondly, the pace at which earnings in the various job categories have risen (see Table 3). One will notice immediately that the number of those without any occupation, who for the most part live off old-age pensions, has risen since 1950 (and, as we have already seen, will continue to rise). This group forms about 14 per cent of the population. 41·4 per cent of the population (mainly women and children) are dependents, earning no money themselves. Our interest for the moment is, however,

Table 2   Occupational status and source of income

	as % of the population	as % of the total of employed persons	as % of the population	as % of the total of employed persons
	*1950**		*1968†*	
Self-employed:				
Entrepreneurs, independent professions and farmers	6·8	14·8	4·9	11·2
Members of families who assist the above (particularly in farming)	6·7	14·4	3·5	7·9
Employees:				
Civil Servants	1·8	4·0	2·4	5·4
White-collar workers	7·4	16·0	12·6	28·2
Workers	23·5	50·8	21·0	47·3
Total number of employed persons	46·3	100·0	44·6	100·0
Independent persons without a job (especially pensioners)	12·0		14·0	
Members of families of employed persons and 'independents' out of work	41·7		41·4	

	in thousands	
Population	47,696	60,065
Employed persons	22,074	26,766
Self-employed and assistants (see above)	6,442	5,113
Employees	15,632	21,655
Persons without employment	25,621	33,298

Calculated according to *Statistisches Jahrbuch* (1954), p. 114; (1969), p. 121 and p. 124.

* Without the Saar and West Berlin.   † By microcensus (estimated figures).

directed to the 44·6 per cent of the population who are gainfully employed.

The numbers of self-employed, i.e. entrepreneurs, members of independent professions and farmers, together with the members of their families who help them in their business, have gone down from 30 per cent of the working population in 1950 to 20 per cent in 1968. The number of employed persons has increased proportionately. This reflects the increasing industrialization and the trend to economic concentration.

The following table shows income growth over approximately the same period; it will be noted that, although the earnings of employed persons have risen considerably, they have not risen nearly as steeply as the earnings of employers.

Table 3   Income growth

(Expressed: (*a*) as average earnings for each year in West German marks (DM); (*b*) as compared with average income in 1950)

	1950	*1955*	*1959*	*1963*	*1967*
Employees	(*a*) 2544	(*a*) 3767	(*a*) 4781	(*a*) 6471	(*a*) 8388
	(*b*) 100	(*b*) 148	(*b*) 188	(*b*) 254	(*b*) 330
Entrepreneurs and self-employed together with members of the family who assist them	(*a*) 3030	(*a*) 5100	(*a*) 7103	(*a*) 10,644	(*a*) 15,106
	(*b*) 100	(*b*) 168	(*b*) 234	(*b*) 351	(*b*) 499

According to Bruno Gleitze, *Sozialkapital und Sozialfonds als Mittel der Vermögenspolitik* (Köln, 1968).

If one expresses the combined sum of public and private wealth in the GFR in the year 1950 as 100, this sum rose (over twenty times) to 2153 in 1967. (In 1967 one-third of the nation's wealth was publicly owned.) In the area of private ownership the class of employers increased its wealth, as we have seen, more quickly than employees. If one expresses the wealth in the hands of this employer class as 100 in the year 1950, by 1967 it had risen to 2210, whereas that of employees together with pensioners had only risen from 100 to 983 over the same period. Looking at the same situation from another angle, it is significant that even though in 1950 the proportion of ownership of private wealth was already 53 : 47 (self-employed first, employees and pensioners second), by 1967 the scales had tipped more sharply still in favour of the former: 72 : 28. These figures become even more significant when one considers that there are about five times as many employees and pensioners as self-employed. It is only recently that dissatisfaction at this disproportionate wealth distribution has begun to spread. One of the reasons for this is the gradual generation change-over that we examined earlier. The older people who had gone through the war and had suffered a great deal were at once so pleased about, and yet so concerned for, the growing prosperity, that they tended not to think about whether it was fairly distributed. The experiences of the Cold War, the all-too-apparent political repression of the population of the Socialist states in eastern Europe and their much lower standard of living, together with the growing respect which the new state enjoyed in the other West European and North Atlantic societies with a similar fundamental social order, all helped to make people unaware of underlying developments in the GFR. In addition, the accumulation of wealth was masked by the high level of investment (i.e. profits being put back into the business where they were made, instead of being spent by business and state), or came to light only in the idiosyncratic behaviour of certain prominent people which met with general disapproval.

Opportunities for Educational and Social Advancement

In the GFR, as in all modern societies based on the individual's ability to get ahead by his own efforts (*Leistungsgesellschaften*), it is the level of education attained, rather than family background, that opens the door to positions of responsibility. Table 4 represents a sample of managers in West German industry. Most of them come not from the upper class or upper middle class, in fact more than half are of lower middle class or working class origin (though only a very small percentage comes

from the latter class). 62·5 per cent of them, however, have a
university or *Technische Hochschule* (technical university)
education and 26·1 per cent have at least attended high school
(*höhere Schule*).

*Table 4 Social origin and educational attainments of 537
managers in West German industry*
(expressed as a percentage)

	Managers	Their fathers	Their grandfathers
Upper class	100·0	16·2	4·3
Upper middle class	—	29·2	21·4
Lower middle class	—	49·5	62·9
Working class	—	5·1	11·4
Completed *Volksschule*	5·8	46·7	68·7
Completed *Mittelschule*	5·6		
Completed *höhere Schule*	26·1	31·3	17·2
Completed university or *Technische Hochschule*	62·5	21·7	8·8
No details given	—	0·3	5·3

According to Stephanie Münke, *Die mobile Gesellschaft* (Stuttgart,
1967), p. 146 ff.

Another sample survey of various *élites* in the GFR, carried
out by W. Zapf, is revealing. According to this, high-ranking
lawyers and secretaries of state, ambassadors and generals,
leaders of industrial combines and big businessmen, editors-in-
chief and broadcasting intendants come mainly from the upper
middle class, indeed some of them belong to the aristocracy.
Ministers and heads of the *Länder*, parliamentary leaders, party
chiefs and church prelates come, for the most part, from the
middle class, while trade-union bosses come from the upper
levels of the working class. One can see from the table that this
is a society in which the individual can rise through his own
efforts. However, being 'well-born' is still indirectly of great
importance in the attainment of positions of great responsibility

in that it provides the opportunity and the incentive for a good education. This is clear in Table 5.

Table 5   Students at West German universities grouped according to the occupation and educational background of their fathers (expressed as a percentage)

Fathers' occupation	1949–1950[1]	1964–1965[2]	Percentage of the total population in May 1965[3]
Civil servants	40·3	32·9	5·0
White-collar workers	18·4	30·3 ⎫	
Independent professions	12·9	12·6 ⎭	26·3
Farmers and peasants	5·0	3·3	11·6
Those involved in trade and commerce	18·3	14·2 ⎫	
Workers	4·4	5·3 ⎭	48·7
Other professions	0·7	0·5	8·4*
Without an occupation or no occupation given	—	0·9	—
Academic background	28·7	35·4	—
No academic background	71·3	65·5	—

* Includes members of the family who assist in the work.
According to:
[1] *Statistische Berichte*, Arbeits Nr. VIII/4/7, *Statistisches Bundesamt Wiesbaden*, v. 15.2.51.
[2] *Statistisches Bundesamt Wiesbaden*, Reihe 10, *Bildungswesen*, V. Hochschulen (1964–5).
[3] *Statistisches Jahrbuch* (1967), p. 138.

Although in 1965 employees made up 48·7 per cent of the working population, their children represented only 5·3 per cent of the West German student population. Civil Servants make up only 5 per cent of the working population and yet 32·9 per cent of all students come from the families of Civil Servants. A comparison between 1949–50 and 1964–5 shows a remarkable increase in the numbers of students who are the children of white-collar workers. The trend is most apparent in the *decreasing* numbers of students whose fathers have no academic background. So we can see that it is still true that children with a middle or upper class background will tend to get a better education and will also have greater opportunities for social advancement.

We must not forget that education is not simply a passport to a good job, but something valuable in itself. The following table leaves the question of social origin aside and presents the educational situation in the simplest terms. It shows that only 5 per cent of the total population qualify for university and, at the other end of the scale, 76 per cent of the population have fulfilled only the minimum educational requirements:

Table 6   Educational level attained at time of leaving school
(expressed as a percentage)

	1954	1967
Volksschule (basic schooling)	84	76
Mittlere Reife (more advanced secondary education)	12	19
Abitur (qualification for University)	4	5

According to research done by the Institut für Demoskopie Allensbach, in the *Jahrbuch der öffentlichen Meinung 1965-7* (Allensbach und Bonn, 1967), p. 4.

Special Problems of Young and Old People

The lack of educational planning and facilities led one critic to talk of 'the German educational catastrophe' (*die deutsche Bildungskatastrophe*). There is a serious shortage of kindergartens, school rooms, teachers and facilities for study or for professional training. The young are finding themselves caught in a dilemma. On the one hand, a fast developing economy requires people with specialized technical qualifications, which take a longer training period and correspondingly postpone the time at which the young person is considered to have reached maturity; on the other hand, because of the omissions of the educational system sketched above, it is largely left to the business and professional world to bridge the gap created. This it does, as one might expect, according to its own narrow criteria of efficiency. Thus, for most young people for whom no room can be found in the high school or university system, there is a transition period between the end of their schooling and the beginning of their working life, during which time they are much sought after as a cheap source of labour. In this period they are gradually absorbed into the work-force and must face the anxious situation of competing with their fellows for qualifications and the attention of the entrepreneurs. Even if they have started a family of their own they are not treated as responsible adults.

The situation of the old people is also unenviable. Their problems are different from those of the young but are also connected with the present capitalist structure of society where competition between various kinds of private enterprise is the dominant principle (the technical term is: *privatkapitalistische Leistungskonkurrenzgesellschaft*). It is not usually admitted, but unfortunately it is a fact, that the old people in West German society are widely considered to be a burden because not only do they not contribute to the economy, but they also need assistance from it. As people get older (from forty-five onwards, in fact) it becomes more and more difficult for them to find a suitable post if they change jobs. Retired people find that they have too little money and that social and medical care is inadequate. Tables 7 and 8 show the economic situation of old people.

74·2 per cent of all the households, which in 1962–3 had incomes of less than DM 300 a month, were pensioners; 41·9 per cent of all pensioner households belonged to this group. One must remember that, in some cases, the income scarcely guaranteed even the bare minimum needed to live, let alone provided the basis for a civilized existence: in 1962, 14·3 per cent of social insurance pensioners (6·8 per cent of the men and

Table 7   Net monthly income of pensioner households 1962–1963

Income groups	Proportion of all households in this income group (in %)	Proportion of all pensioner households (in %)
Under DM 300	74·2	41·9
DM 300–600	26·8	39·4
DM 600–800	12·4	10·9
DM 800–1200	9·7	6·0
DM 1200 and above	6·1	1·8

According to *Soziale Sicherung in der BRD*, A Social Survey, Anlagenband (Stuttgart o.J.), p. 65.

20·5 per cent of the women) had a monthly income of less than DM 150. It is small wonder that a large percentage of those over sixty-five were unable to retire, as is shown in Table 8.

It is true that after 1959 pensions were increased to keep step with rises in the incomes of wage-earners (in 1968 the rise was 8·1 per cent) but this did nothing to close the gap which had grown wider and wider before 1959. The situation of pensioners has scarcely improved at all since the last time information was made available. In February 1969, the average income of retired workers was DM 324·75 and that of retired white-collar workers was DM 541·99.

Table 8   Old people over sixty-five still in employment in 1961 (expressed as a percentage of this age-group)

Age	Men	Women
65–70	32·6	12·2
70–75	21·4	7·4
Over 75	11·2	3·5

According to *Soziale Sicherung in der BRD*, A Social Survey, Anlagenband (Stuttgart o.J.), p. 59.

Political Trends

Table 9 shows the proportion of votes cast for the various parties in the *Bundestag* and *Landtage* elections since 1949. The trend towards a three-party or even a two-party system is quite apparent. This development has increasingly obscured the underlying association of parties with particular social classes.

Table 9   *Votes cast for the various parties in the* Bundestag (BT) *and* Landtage (LTe) *elections since 1949*
(expressed as a percentage of the total vote).

	BT 1949	BT 1953	LTe 1953–6	BT 1957	LTe 1957–60	BT 1961	LTe 1961–4	BT 1965	LTe 1965–8	BT 1969
Numbers of those entitled to vote (in millions)	31	33	34	35	36	37	38	38	38·6	38
Percentage vote	78·5	86·0	75·5	87·8	76·4	87·7	74·6	86·8	76·6	86·8
Percentage of valid votes for:										
CDU/CSU	31·0	45·0	33·0	50·2	37·5	45·4	39·0	47·6	39·8	46·1
SPD	29·2	28·8	34·1	31·8	40·2	36·2	43·4	39·3	43·0	42·7
FDP	11·9	9·5	10·3	7·7	8·8	12·8	9·6	9·5	8·4	5·8
GVP*	6·1	9·8	9·3	9·2	8·2	2·6	2·2	—	0·5	—
Left-wing splinter parties†	6·0	2·1	3·4	—	n.d.§	2·2	n.d.	1·7	n.d.	0·6
Right-wing splinter parties‡	0·8	1·6	0·6	0·3	1·6	—	n.d.	2·2	5·8	4·3
Other parties and independent members of Parliament	10·6	2·6	9·3	0·8	3·8	0·2	5·8	0·0	2·5	0·5

* 1949–57 *DP* (*Deutsche Partei*) and *BHE*, later *GVP* (*Gesamtdeutsche Volkspartei*).
† 1949–53 especially *KPD* (*Kommunistische Partei Deutschlands*) banned in 1955.
‡ 1949–53 especially *DRP* (*Deutsche Reichspartei*) from 1965 *NPD* (*Nationaldemokratische Partei Deutschlands*).
§ No details available.

Calculated according to *Statistisches Jahrbuch* (Abt. VI Wahlen), 1953, 1957, 1961, 1965, 1969; and Heft 272b of the *Beiträge zur Statistik Bayerns* (Bayerisches Statistisches Landesamt, 1969), p. 169 ff.

The groups of the decidedly nationalistic *Deutsche Partei* (*DP*) and the *Block der Heimatvertriebenen und Entrechteten* (*BHE*) which, up to the end of the fifties, were able to unite to form the fourth largest party (the *Gesamtdeutsche Volkspartei – GVP*) have gone the way of many parties which were of some importance when the GFR was founded and have, like them, to a large extent been absorbed by the three main parties (except where they became a reservoir for the new *National Democratic Party* (*NPD*) which is already on the wane). Through this trend to the two-party system the parties have begun to appeal to all sections of the public – this is particularly noticeable in election campaigns. It is still perhaps true that the workers preserve something of their affinity for the *SPD* and the middle class for the *CDU* and the *FDP*. But since the *SPD* changed its policies at the Bad Godesberg Party Conference in 1959 to become a people's party, the parties have ceased to make their objectives clearly accord with those of a particular class. The political parties tend to comprise a number of diverse factions so that the composition of the individual party precludes a clearly defined party programme.

Participation in Politics

Table 10 indicates how many people take an active part in public affairs and it will help us to see to what extent West Germany has really become a participatory democracy. It is true that the Basic Law guarantees the freedom to form political parties and interest groups which, or so the theory goes, can exert their influence on the organs of government. However, politically active people are in a very small minority and, in practical terms, the situation seems to be as follows: a mass of passive citizens, on the one hand, is confronted by the 'establishment' apparatus of the state, the parties and other organizations, on the other (the latter only 'polarizing' to express minor differences in points of view at election time). Since a participatory democracy embraces more than party politics alone, the issue of workers' participation in management is relevant here.

Workers' 'Co-determination' (*Mitbestimmung*)

An ever-increasing percentage of the working population is employed in large firms. In 1950, 37·3 per cent worked in businesses with fewer than ten employees, in 1961 the figure was only 25·7 per cent; in 1950, 17·6 per cent of the working population were in businesses with more than 500 employees whereas in 1961 this proportion had risen to 23·2 per cent. In view of this

Table 10   Participation in public life

	In thousands	As a percentage
Members of Parliament in *Bund* and *Länder*	1·6	0·04
Members of parish councils (*Gemeinderäte*) and Parliaments (*Kreistage*)	220·0	0·6
Members of political parties	1200·0	3·1
Those who occasionally take part in some kind of political activity	5000·0	13·1
Union members	6500·0	17·1
Regular churchgoers	13,000·0	34·2
Members of clubs and other organizations	15,000·0	39·5
Readers of regional newspapers	25,000·0	65·8
Voters at *Landtage* elections	27,000·0	71·0
Voters at *Bundestag* elections	34,000·0	89·4
Those entitled to vote	38,000·0	100·0

After W. Hartenstein and K. Liepelt, 'Mitglieder und Wähler', in F. Sänger and K. Liepelt, *Wahlhandbuch 1965*, Part 2, p. 33. These figures refer to the year 1961–2 but have not since changed substantially.

development it is important to find out what kind of relationship exists, in a given enterprise, between the owner and management on the one hand, and the workers on the other.

After the war there were two opposing conceptions of co-determination (i.e. the workers having a say in the running of the business where they work). In the Marxist-orientated view, co-determination was a weapon in the class struggle which, by limiting capitalist control of the means of production, would eventually allow workers to run their factories themselves. Supporters with Social Democrat leanings saw in co-determination an opportunity for 'training in democracy' at the place of work, expecting, firstly, that such habits would spread to other areas of society, and, secondly, that this would prevent economic power being transformed into political power.

In the early post-war years the unions and the *SPD* were by no means alone in their demand for co-determination. The churches and the *CDU* also gave their support. Even the constitutions of some of the *Länder* contained articles to this effect. The entrepreneurs were at this early stage ready to co-operate because everyone was involved in the rebuilding of factories and workshops. This spirit of co-operation flourished *before* the founding of the GFR, having originated with the publication of the Allies' plans for reparations and the German industrial levels. These plans met with the resistance of German management and workers alike – the latter fearing for their jobs. Thus, at the negotiations with the Allies about dismantlings, workers as well as management were represented.

Hopes for an 'economic democracy' rose with the developments in the iron and steel industry in the Ruhr. This was being broken into smaller units (*entflochten*) to crush the political might which had greatly assisted the rise of the Nazi regime and helped to establish it firmly in power. Five members of the supervisory council (*Aufsichtsrat*) of each enterprise concerned represented the entrepreneurs; three of these were put forward by the individual concern; another representative with entrepreneurial sympathies came from the Civil Service and another came from the management of the companies which had been broken up (usually one of the works managers). Five other members of the *Aufsichtsrat* represented the interests of the employees; two of these were members of the individual *Betriebsrat* (see below), two representatives came from the unions and the other was chosen from the Civil Service on the recommendation of the unions. The *Aufsichtsrat* chose the management of each organization which usually comprised three executives; one of these, the managing director, was supported by the employer-representatives and was primarily responsible for social and personnel matters. These arrangements were given the authority of the law in the Mining Industry's Co-Determination Law (*Mitbestimmungsgesetz*) passed in 1951.

The law concerning the organization of all other sections of industry (*Betriebsverfassungsgesetz*) passed in 1952, which is still in force today, was only a watered-down version of this earlier law. According to it, workers' representatives can lay claim to only one-third of the seats in the *Aufsichtsrat* and union representatives who are not employed by the particular firm are only allowed if there are more than nine members on the council and the particular firm is not a family business. The *Betriebsrat*, which represents the interests of the workers in a given firm, has a say in little more than the welfare of those it represents. Its influence on issues such as the policy of the firm, is very limited. Because the *Mitbestimmungsgesetz* of the mining industry was not extended to the rest of the economy, the old structures, where industry was privately owned and run, were gradually re-established. They have been defended on grounds of economic efficiency but they have in fact led to the development of alternatives to a fully democratic form of society.

'Regimented Society' (*Formierte Gesellschaft*) or Social Democracy?

Our original question was whether the development of West German social structures up till now can be seen as the realization of a constitutional democracy in a just society. It is true that this society is radically different from the Weimar Republic from which National Socialism had sprung. However the re-birth of a society with a definite class structure, which was certainly not considered desirable in 1945–6 and which for that reason must not be seen as an inevitable development, is unmistakable. One must recognize that this process, unfolding within the structures of a pluralistic democracy, has in fact become a danger for those same structures – this has been evident ever since the emergence of a new ideology, the 'regimented society' (*formierte Gesellschaft*), a term coined by interim *CDU* Chancellor Erhard, which was adopted by those who were particularly interested in the preservation of class structures.

Meanwhile the opposition movement among the young intellectuals and the unions has made clear the dangers involved above all in the constitutional changes brought about by the emergency legislation (*Notstandsgesetzgebung*) in 1968: this might be misused to create that *formierte Gesellschaft* where both opposition movements that are now protesting against class distinctions would be suppressed, and also constitutional rights which are now upheld, would be abolished. But since, in the meantime, the Social Democrat Party in league with the Liberals has succeeded in banishing the Christian Democratic Union into opposition – hopes for a change in this situation have been strengthened. Whether the new government, which is weighed down with the burden of expectations placed on it, will be able both to make at least partial structural changes and to make participation, and thus co-determination, possible in all sections of society, only the future will tell. The term 'constitutional social democracy' (*rechtstaatliche und soziale Demokratie*) does not describe the present situation in West Germany; it does however provide a measure by which anyone who is anxious to establish democracy firmly within the GFR, can judge the present situation.

The Development of Society in the German Democratic Republic

In the following pages we shall briefly examine the GDR's claim to offer a superior social alternative to the GFR.

As in the case of the GFR, it was during the occupation that guidelines for the future development of the GDR were laid down. But here denazification involved more drastic changes. Even though this hampered the rebuilding of the economy, the administration and the educational system, the GDR rejected many qualified people, because of their bourgeois background and affiliations, in favour of less well-trained but politically acceptable staff. Measures such as the state take-over, without any compensation, of all heavy industry and large estates, meant an even greater social upheaval than in the GFR. Ownership of industry was transferred from private individuals to the state and, by 1956, 85 per cent of industry was in state hands and the whole apparatus of industrial and agricultural management was reorganized. In this restructuring of social and political life, the lead was taken by the increasingly Communist-dominated *SED* (*Sozialistische Einheitspartei Deutschlands*) which was formed in 1946 by the enforced merger of the Communist and Social Democrat parties. This party became the main instrument of the Soviet occupation forces and by enforcing a 'national front' with all other parties secured a monopoly over the bourgeois parties which had been revived in 1945. When the GDR came into existence, shortly after the GFR, the *SED* became the official state party and was able to make use of the full apparatus of the state in its attempts to implement socialist policies. However, although it has succeeded in radically transforming the state, it has not accomplished what it set out to do. There were several reasons why it failed to gain widespread support among the population: in the early stages of the regime, harsh authoritarian methods were used; the new state quite openly sacrificed its own interests in favour of the policies of the Soviet Union and, in addition, it came off poorly when compared with West Germany with its pluralistic party system and 'economic miracle'. Thus the *SED* was forced to rely more and more heavily on its reshaping of social institutions and on ideological propaganda which attempted to change the outlook and attitudes of the citizens of the GDR and, in particular, the younger generation and the working class. A proof of how difficult this task was, can be found in the revolt of the GDR population in 1953 and the constant stream of refugees leaving the country which was only stemmed when the Berlin Wall was built and border guards were ordered to fire on anyone who attempted to cross the border without permission. The authoritarian structures developed in the GDR were more rigid and unbending than in other East European Communist countries and made the transformation of the state into a socialist society a hollow boast. It must not be overlooked that great socio-political changes have been effected; the GDR has also had its 'economic miracle' – though several years later than the GFR – and its standard of living is higher than that of the Soviet Union. Indeed, the new state can be said to have come to terms with its Communist leaders and to have made the decisive break with bourgeois-capitalist traditions at the time when the economic revival began. It is by no means a classless society, and certainly not a non-authoritarian society, but it has developed its own unique social order. Positions of great responsibility go to those with the requisite educational qualifications and personal record; the way to such positions is scrupulously kept open to all. One's social origin is not taken into consideration.

Instead, social level is linked to one's individual qualifications. 15–20 per cent of the population – those who were unable to satisfy the minimum educational requirements – make up the lower classes. They are, for the most part, unskilled or semi-skilled workers. The upper class, the new intelligentsia – administrators and lawyers, industrial and agricultural economists, engineers, chemists, doctors and teachers – is not much smaller in number than the lower class. Between these two poles is the mass of skilled workers making up about two-thirds of the total work-force. Since private ownership has been reduced to negligible proportions, all employed persons including trainees are, so to speak, public-service workers; they belong to a huge network of state-run industries, agricultural collectives, public trade organizations (*Handelsorganisationen*) and public educational and welfare services.

Members of the new intelligentsia enjoy certain privileges. They can negotiate better pay and employment contracts than average workers; their old-age security benefits are higher and study opportunities for their children are greater. The abolition of the 'class society' does not mean that the socio-economic situation of different groups within the society is identical. The system of values is certainly different from that existing in

108

THE STRUCTURE OF GERMAN SOCIETY

Western societies. The production worker has a much higher social 'rating' and 50 per cent of students at universities come from the working classes. The individual is much more closely involved with various collectives: his place of work, the neighbourhood where he lives, the youth group, union and cultural club where he is active. He is thus exposed to a greater degree of social control and interference but, on the positive side, this social arrangement does provide protection and assistance. The society of the GDR offers a combination of greater social security and equality than in the GFR but simultaneously exerts a number of pressures: the need to improve one's qualifications constantly, to produce peak performances all the time, and of course, to conform to the dictates of those who wield political power. Above all there is not room for any kind of political nonconformism, let alone the organized opposition of Western democracies. The result is that the mass media are slavishly conformist and uninspired, as indeed is the whole cultural scene. However, with the generation shift in the GDR, the present passive acceptance of the situation is changing to a sense of belonging to the new society. There is a widespread sense of pride in hard-won economic and social advances. This pride will grow as long as it continues to be necessary to come to terms with the present environment – time is on its side.

The claim to be a Socialist people's democracy, and so to have steered a better course than the GFR, is not borne out by the actual situation in the GDR. It is true that, as a result of the inefficiency of centralized administration, the responsibility for some economic planning has been delegated to the state-owned factories and works-collectives, and that the citizens of the GDR tend, through various bodies, to become more intensively involved in local, industrial and communal administration of planning decisions which have been made by the government, than those of the GFR. However, there is still no effective check on fundamental political decisions taken by the regime. The GDR offers democratic socialism, where the whole society takes part in political decision-making, in name only. Like the GFR, this society is not what it claims to be. Unfortunately the competition of ideologies between the two state systems makes any sober and unbiased comparison extraordinarily difficult and is thus detrimental to the development of both societies.

(Completed in February 1970)

Select Bibliography

WOLFGANG ABENDROTH, *Antagonistische Gesellschaft und politische Demokratie* (Neuwied, 1967).

DIETER CLAESSENS, ARNO KLÖNNE and ARMIN TSCHOEPE, *Sozialkunde der BRD* (Düsseldorf, 1965).

RALF DAHRENDORF, *Gesellschaft und Demokratie in Deutschland* (München, 1965).

ERNST DÄUERLEIN, *DDR, Geschichte und Bestandsaufnahme* (München, 1966).

JOHN DORNBERG, *The Other Germany* (Garden City, N.Y., 1968).

FRIEDRICH FÜRSTENBERG, *Die Sozialstruktur der BRD* (Köln-Opladen, 1967).

ALFRED GROSSER, *The Federal Republic of Germany* (London, 1964). (Translated from the French.)

ARTHUR M. HANHARDT, JR, *The German Democratic Republic* (Baltimore, 1968).

ARNOLD HEIDENHEIMER, *The Governments of Germany* (New York, 1961).

RICHARD HISCOCKS, *Germany Revived* (London, 1966).

URS JAEGGI, *Macht und Herrschaft in der Bundesrepublik* (Frankfurt, 1969).

ERNST RICHERT, *Das zweite Deutschland – DDR* (Frankfurt, 1966).

5 Germany: Economic Developments, Problems and Policies[1]

M. E. STREIT

On the following pages only a highly selective analysis of the German economy, or rather the German economies, has been possible. We shall concentrate on economic history since the thirties, with special emphasis on problems of general economic policy.

Reorganization of the German Economy during the Third Reich: The Totalitarian Way

The Nazi economy was not organized systematically according to preconceived plans. It emerged gradually from the problems which were created by the policy of self-sufficiency and independence from world markets. In the early years of the Nazi regime, Hitler repeatedly emphasized the importance of economic freedom, but this did not prevent him from reducing this freedom step by step. In 1938, when the regime considered Germany ready for war, hardly any traces of a free market economy (where the basic problems of what and how much is to be produced and also where and how it is to be produced are solved through the interplay of supply and demand decisions of free consumers and producers and not determined by the government) were left. Wage controls and compulsory allocation of labour, a foreign trade reduced to bilateralism (i.e. barter agreements on trade between the Reich and individual

[1] I am most grateful to the editor as well as to W. E. Kasper and H. Müller-Groeling (Kiel, Germany) and to K. F. Stegemann (Kingston, Ontario) for their criticisms and suggestions.

foreign countries), a state-controlled banking system, an agricultural sector cartelized by law (the term 'cartel' normally refers to agreements among competing enterprises to restrain trade to the disadvantage of consumers by excluding price competition, fixing production quotas, etc.), and investment as well as production controls in other sectors of the economy, clearly indicate the totalitarian character of the Nazi economic system.

There are many reasons why the Germans did not object vigorously to being led along 'the road to serfdom' until it was too late. From an economic point of view one has to take into account: (i) that the First World War reparations had implied a heavy economic burden which most Germans considered unjust, a view supported by Nazi propaganda; (ii) that the Great Depression (6 million unemployed at its peak in Germany) had discredited the free enterprise system; and (iii) that prevalent, authoritarian prejudices seemed to be confirmed by the success of the government's job-creation programme which was started immediately after the seizure of power by Hitler in 1933. For the glamour of the well-kept promise of 'work and bread' it was irrelevant that this programme had a (small-sized) forerunner in the Weimar Republic, that it was started in the time of world-wide recovery, and that it was by no means a National Socialist invention.

Backed by public sympathy after an almost immediate drop in unemployment, by militant party organizations, and by a running fire of propaganda, the first attack on basic rights was quickly launched. Ironically enough the day after Labour Day, 1933, the trade unions were forcibly dissolved; many union leaders had to pay a heavy price for their opposition to Hitler. Blue- and white-collar workers, managers and the professional classes alike had to accept that from now on they would be represented by the so-called 'Work Front' (*Arbeitsfront*), a National Socialist party organization. The legal basis for a strict wage control was finally provided in 1934 when the 'Law of Regulation of National Labour' (*Gesetz zur Ordnung der nationalen Arbeit*) established what was called the 'leadership principle' (*Führerprinzip*) in labour relations. Though it was labelled as introducing a patriarchal relationship between employers and employees, supervised by a 'Trustee of Labour' (*Treuhänder der Arbeit*), a party official, it turned out to be the institutional framework for full state control. In practical terms the *Treuhänder* had unlimited power to dictate all conditions of work, as his decisions superseded any pre-existing arrangements. Free mobility of labour was abolished in 1935 with the introduction of a 'Labour Book' (*Arbeitsbuch*) as a formal prerequisite for any employment. At first, mobility was only restricted in so far as an employer could refuse to hand the book back to the employee, forcing the employee to continue in his present job. But after 1938 the government was entitled by law to shift workers from one place to another at its discretion.

As part of the self-sufficiency programme, agriculture had to be reorganized. As early as the summer of 1933 all persons who had anything at all to do with agriculture became members of a kind of statutory cartel, the 'Reich Food Estate' (*Reichsnährstand*). Marketing boards fixed prices, regulated supplies, and set production quotas. Hardly anything was left to the initiative of the individual farmer. But, despite all efforts, the goal of self-sufficiency remained out of reach.

Like the farms, factories continued, for the most part, under the ownership of private individuals and companies, but the owners were no longer free to make their own business decisions. In 1934, the 'Law to Prepare the Organic Reconstruction of the German Economy' (*Gesetz zur Vorbereitung des organischen Aufbaus der deutschen Wirtschaft*) gave the regime authority to reorganize industry and trade in a sort of super-cartel. It was a merger of pre-existing, private, monopolistic organizations and state power. Many of those who had been in charge of cartels – and the number of cartels, which an official estimate in 1920 had put at 2500, had not decreased in the meantime – became chairmen of 'Economic Groups' (*Reichsgruppen*). They had to coordinate industrial production according to the government's directives. Many employers were quite willing (in contrast to the unions) to co-operate with a regime which initially suited their authoritarian tendencies and promised sure profits.

A further element of control was forced upon the economy as a consequence of balance of payments problems which accompanied the German recovery. In the wake of the Great Depression, all leading industrial countries, except Germany, had devalued their currencies. Now the Reichsmark seemed to be hopelessly overvalued, and this fostered imports and handicapped exports. Export-competitiveness deteriorated further as a result of the drive to introduce substitutes for foreign raw materials, which were produced at home by expensive techniques. The resulting disequilibrium in foreign trade and the shortage of currency reserves were covered up by controlling the allocation of foreign exchange. Foreign trade was monopolized by the state and controlled by a system of bilateral trade agreements, import licensing and export subsidies.

Financing and directing the job-creation programme, the self-sufficiency experiments and rearmament, required control over the whole banking system. This was brought about by law in 1934. The fact that government debts rose steeply despite increasing taxation and special revenues from the expropriation of foreign creditors was veiled by financing these debts with short-term bills revolved by special financing agencies. After 1935 budgets and records of the Reich debt were simply no longer published.

Wage controls and, in 1936, a general wage and price stop were the answer to inflationary pressures. That they had already made themselves felt at a time when the German economy was producing below potential output (in 1936 more than one million were still unemployed) resulted from the unbalanced and inefficient use of national resources. The job-creation programme tended to stress the building and related industries, the struggle for self-sufficiency in food and industrial raw materials swallowed a considerable amount of scarce resources and the rearmament programme led to shortages of skilled labour as early as 1936. The government's costly plans required an ever-

114

growing portion of the total national product. Only a wage and price freeze could help to disguise the growing absorption of resources by the state and avoid open inflation or excessive taxation. Consequently employment increased but the standard of living did not rise much above the 1928 level.

Only slowly and in a process of trial and error were the above elements of government control integrated into a system of central planning of the economy. For a long time private activity was controlled primarily via the allocation of investment funds; attractive profit margins for required products were offered (as a basis for self-financing), and priorities were given to the purchase of the necessary materials. For the first few years, the economic system was a government-regulated (dirigistic) economy rather than a planned economy after the socialist pattern. Things did not change significantly with the first four-year plan which was introduced in 1936 as the latest achievement of National Socialism. Difficulties not unknown in Eastern socialist economies arose soon after the price stop of 1936. As the frozen prices did not act as an indicator of developing scarcities, they lost their economic function of rationing and controlling production and cost, and prejudiced the efficient use of resources. Allocation of materials became increasingly a matter of rivalry between producer groups, backed by different members of the Nazi leadership.

Economic Problems of the War: From *Blitzkrieg* to Total War

Although state control over the economy was considerable in 1939, the economy as such cannot be described as a war economy. Until 1937, government expenditure on armament had only risen from 5·5 to 9·6 per cent of the national product. It was only in 1938 that this figure shot up to more than 18 per cent. At the outbreak of the war, Germany's potential opponents grossly overestimated her lead over them. A large quantity of arms of high quality was available but the armament-production capacity was small and inadequate for a lengthy war. This situation corresponded to the concept of *Blitzkrieg*, a quick knock-out strategy. If successful, it obviated hardships like those borne by the civilian population during the long First World War. And for the first two years, the concept of 'guns and butter' seemed to work; the greater mass-production potential of the Reich's opponents did not come into play.

While the German army was advancing and exploiting the resources of defeated countries, and while Allied bombing was moderate, the fundamental vulnerability of the German economy remained hidden. It was even possible to tolerate a rather inefficient armament production, considerably misguided by rivalry within the party leadership, by uncoordinated decision-making on different weapons and by poorly co-ordinated allocation of resources (especially labour). The success of the Polish and French offensives seemed to suggest that no further exertions were necessary. As a consequence, armament production stagnated at the 1940 level until 1942. Hardly any arms plant worked more than one shift and working time was scarcely above peacetime levels. Rationing of consumer goods was only slowly extended. But after America's entry into the war at the end of 1941, and the first set-backs during the Russian winter campaign of 1941–2, the need for adjustment to a long war became pressing.

The new strategy, propagated at the beginning of 1942, was an attempt to offset the mass production of the Allies by superior quality armament. At the same time arms production was thoroughly reorganized by the Ministry for Armament and Munitions. German industry revealed unforeseen productivity reserves. From February 1942 to February 1943, total armament production was more than doubled; in summer 1944, it was three times as high as at the beginning of 1942. But the losses of equipment became heavier too, creating not only replacement demand but also reducing the effects of superior quality armaments. Supplies of largely imported, strategic raw materials like iron-ore, non-ferrous metals and petrol became

116

drastically short when the German troops were thrown back from foreign territory and when factories and communication lines were under almost continuous air attack. As to manpower, it became necessary to boost supply by proclaiming 'total war' as early as January 1943, making all men between the ages of sixteen and sixty-five, and all women from seventeen to forty-five, subject to conscription.

When it became evident that superiority could not be achieved by better quality armaments, the last hopes of survival lay in mass production of existing types of weapons and an enlarged army. But, in 1944, raw materials were already in short supply, the loss of industrial area in the West could not be made good, and reinforcements of the *Wehrmacht* meant an even more serious labour shortage in arms industries.

Total Defeat: The Rubble of the Third Reich

With the loss of the heavy industries of the Ruhr in March 1945, the economic and military catastrophe was complete. But if the 'Fortress Germany' (*Festung Deutschland*) could not be defended, Hitler decided that the advancing enemy should find a wasteland. Fortunately, the 'scorched-earth strategy' (*Strategie der verbrannten Erde*), first considered in 1944, was averted by the Ministry of Armament and Munitions. However, when the Third Reich ceased to exist, war destruction had reached unparalleled dimensions.

Many of Germany's cities were no more than piles of debris with no electricity, water, telephone system, postal service, railway transport, no trade beyond local barter and no administration. In all, about one-fifth of the dwellings were destroyed (in the big cities far more than that). The industrial capital stock was reduced by about the same amount. The economy was deprived of most of its industrial and agricultural supplies. In the Western parts of Germany, the mass of starving and homeless people was further increased by a heavy influx of refugees and expellees from the East.

In contrast to the First World War, Germany was completely conquered by the victors who immediately began to wipe out the traces of the Third Reich. Economically this meant that by industrial disarmament, sweeping decentralization and thorough decartelization, Germany should be prevented from waging future wars. Her economic structure in particular was to be altered fundamentally, by scaling down industrial capacity to a minimum. The dismantling of industrial capacity was to be included in reparations which at Yalta were fixed at a total of 20 billion dollars. (But as early as Potsdam any figure was no longer considered meaningful except by the Soviet Union who insisted on her initial share of 10 billion dollars.) Similarly German property abroad, patent rights, trade-marks and firm-names were used to cover reparation claims. Further compensation was taken out of current production.

The Allies' 'Level of Industry Plan' of 1946 aimed at cutting back German industrial activity drastically, leaving only sufficient capacity to prevent disease and unrest. It prohibited a number of activities completely, restricted the majority of the rest and crippled the few remaining unrestricted branches by shortage of materials. If it had been fully implemented it would have set Germany back to the level of 1932 – or about half of her 1938 capacity.

Post-war Controls: The Bottleneck of European Recovery

At first the Allies appeared to be united in the will to uproot all traces of National Socialism, to punish Germany, to deprive her of all military potential and to make her pay for the damage – this time in kind, in order to avoid the transfer problems which had encumbered the world economy after Versailles. The Soviet Union began at once to dismantle and remove reparation materials to an extent which crippled the productive power of her occupation zone for several years. As dismantling still fell short of the reparations required, Russia interpreted the Yalta agreement on compensation in kind as including parts of Germany's current production. France did not hesitate to follow this example. Both countries received further reparations out of the comparatively more heavily industrialized British and American zones. There, dismantling provoked strikes and agitation. It became obvious that this drain on German capacity and production was far too severe. It was simply self-defeating to withdraw capacity and claim high reparation quotas out of current production which (in industry), in 1946, was less than a quarter of the 1939 level.

After only a single year of occupation, the Allies were almost completely disunited in their policy towards Germany. Whereas the Western powers continued to decentralize, a centralized administration designed to steer a Soviet-type economy was created by Russia in her occupation zone. At the same time political life was manipulated in order to establish a strong Soviet-orientated party organization. The dismantling and the sequestration of large-sized farms and industrial combines under the programme of reparations, demilitarization and denazification provided an opportunity for restructuring the Soviet zone according to socialist principles. At conferences and in the short-lived Allied Control Council, the Soviet Union advocated a unified and centralized Germany, whereas the Western powers continued their decentralization programme; France increased disunity by pressing for separation of the Ruhr from the rest of Germany and for annexation of the Saar region (whose basic industries she had already sequestrated).

At the same time it became more and more obvious, especially in the American and British zones, that the improvised and hopelessly decentralized administration caused economic and social chaos. It delayed and obstructed even the minimum of recovery considered necessary to prevent Germany becoming an international economic burden. But the decisive incentive for corrective steps was political, namely that America finally became aware of Germany's strategic importance in the growing East–West conflict.

In June 1947, the British and American zones were united in the 'United Economic Region' (*Vereinigtes Wirtschaftsgebiet*) with a quasi-parliament on economic matters (*Wirtschaftsrat*), a second chamber (*Länderrat*), and a quasi-government, representing about 40 million Germans. Legislative and administrative competence was limited to economic, financial and social affairs, and decisions were subject to approval by an Anglo-American control board. The 'Level of Industry Plan' was revised but still reflected the old, restrictive mentality.

More and more, the production and capacity restrictions imposed on the German economy held back a general European recovery. The European economy urgently needed reconstruction materials like steel, machinery, chemicals and vehicles which Germany – before the war one of the main European suppliers – was not allowed to produce; and for the products other countries could have provided in exchange, no market existed, since Germany was kept at the subsistence level. Her trade pattern was completely reversed: formerly a leading importer of raw materials, Germany was now exporting her few natural resources. In January 1948, J. F. Dulles, American Secretary of State, declared before a Senate Committee: 'Germany is the bottleneck of European recovery', thereby voicing a conviction which was widespread at the time. In April 1948, the Western zones were included in the European Recovery Programme (Marshall Plan). In all, West Germany received about 1·41 billion dollars under this programme. The aid was used at first to import essential raw materials and food. The equivalent in marks of these imports was accumulated in a special fund which thereafter was used to provide cheap credits to finance, among other things, basic industries, housing and regional development projects.

Currency Reform: The Final Split

The loss of the coal-mines of Silesia and the Saar, the destruction or dismantling of electricity-generating plants, the loss of food supplies from the eastern parts of the former Reich (which were almost completely sealed off), the drastic shortage of housing, and a crippled industry meant that the situation in the Western zones, in the years immediately following the war, was desperate. Starvation on a wide scale was only just averted by American and British measures. In order to avoid complete chaos, the Western Allies had to decide, ironically enough, to preserve virtually the entire apparatus of Nazi economic regulations: freeze on prices, wages and rents, rationing of consumer goods and foodstuffs, allocation of manpower and raw materials, compulsory delivery quotas for farmers, and housing controls.

Since the money supply had been inflated to dizzy heights by the system of war finance, a continuation of the price-stop together with the shortage of nearly everything except money, deprived the Reichsmark of almost all its purchasing power. Payment in kind was the order of the day. No more than half of the total output was subject to official controls at legal prices; the remaining transactions were by barter on the grey and black markets. Enormous, disguised unemployment was another consequence. With food supply sometimes as low as 1000 calories per head per day, farms attracted hordes of hungry city people and refugees offering to do any kind of odd job in return for food. In industry many were kept in jobs with low productivity because they could be paid in nearly worthless Reichsmark at the low rates which had been laid down. A third effect of the archaic controls with unchecked money supply was a distortion of production. Fancy ash-trays, lamp-shades and other baubles that were not subject to price controls, were produced and sold at inflated rates because they were considered a better form of saving than money.

Thorough reforms were postponed by the British and Americans who, clinging to the Potsdam Agreement that Germany should be considered as an economic entity, tried to avoid any step which might lead to division. Three years passed during which hopeless efforts were made to cure Germany's economic diseases. An income taxation, which under normal conditions would have been considered a death-blow to individual initiative, had no noticeable effects, since the amount of money withdrawn via taxation was still too small compared with the vast amount of money in circulation. Plans for a currency reform had been worked out as early as 1946 but endless negotiations with the Soviet Union led nowhere. Despite the pressing need to remove the paralysing and distorting effects of repressed inflation, the decisive step was not taken before Russia cut one of the last ties with her former allies by withdrawing her co-operation from the Allied Control Council in March 1948. After some opposition by France (whom the USA and the UK 'bought off' by accepting the integration of the Saar region into the French economy), the currency reform was finally started on 18 June 1948, introducing a common new currency for the three Western zones, providing the basis for their economic unification, and demarkating the future (1949) Federal Republic. Four days later, the split was made definite by the Soviet occupation forces when they introduced the *Deutsche Mark Ost*.

The basic aims of the currency reform in the West were to reduce money supply and to reorganize public and private debts. The way this was brought about can only be described as successful but unfair when one considers how the economic burden was distributed. Apart from a *per capita* quota of sixty marks as an initial provision of cash (distributed in two stages), all currency and bank deposits, savings included, were cut down to one-fifteenth of their original value (RM 100 = DM 6·5). All private debts were devalued in the ratio 10 : 1, and, in order to prevent enrichment above all through the cancellation of long-term debts, the 'devaluation profit' was taken over by a war damage compensation fund. The huge Reich debt was practically wiped out; in return, private creditors received rather illiquid, low-interest equalization compensation. Although such harsh treatment was meted out to creditors and savers, the holders of real wealth – land, property and industrial shares – got off lightly. The Allies agreed on the need for an 'equalization' of war damages and losses from the currency reform and asked the German representatives to provide a scheme within six months. But it took four years until some legislation was introduced (*Lastenausgleichgesetz* or 'Equalization of Burdens Act'). An equalization levy or tax on private real wealth, spared by war and dismantling, became effective. Although this act would involve collecting the impressive sum of 84 billion marks the problem of the unfair distribution of wealth was not really tackled since the levies to be paid by the wealthy were divided into annual 'mini-instalments', payable until 1979.

Social Market Economy: Capitalism Reintroduced in the West

The economic system which the first West German coalition government claimed to have established under the influence of Professor Erhard, the Minister of Economic Affairs, was labelled 'social market economy' (*Soziale Marktwirtschaft*). Basically, it was supposed to conform to a scientific concept developed by neo-liberal economists including Professors Eucken, von Hayek, and Rüstow. The economic system they proposed is based on private property and private control of resources and is mainly regulated by highly competitive markets. The role of the government is primarily to safeguard competition. Developed at the time of, but in opposition to, the Nazi regime, the doctrine completely rejects government control and planning of the economy. Monetary policy (the amount of money in circulation and the volume of credit lent and borrowed by the private sector is regulated by changes in the bank rate and by changes in the minimum reserves which all credit institutes have to keep as interest-free balances with the central bank; such measures are part of 'monetary policy') plays a central role. It is intended that by keeping the purchasing power of the currency stable through monetary policy, competition in all markets will reduce the business cycle (i.e. the ebb and flow of business activity within an economy over a period of time) to negligible proportions. Anti-cyclical fiscal measures (the government can withdraw purchasing power from the economy, by additional taxation for instance, or can put purchasing power into the economy, e.g. by reducing taxation; thus it can counteract the tendency for demand for goods and services to fluctuate in the private sector; such government measures are described by the term 'anti-cyclical fiscal measures') would be required only on rare occasions. Socially undesirable results of the market mechanism in the field of income and wealth distribution would be corrected by taxation and by a system of social security, without destroying the competitive framework. This theory, which is considered to be neither orthodox *laissez-faire* nor state-dirigism, suggested (i) liberalizing trade in all goods and services as far as is socially justifiable, (ii) introducing a strict anti-trust legislation (to protect competition), (iii) preventing any direct state or pressure-group interference with the market mechanism, and (iv) pursuing a monetary policy leading to steady growth and stable prices.

The decision to return to a basically capitalist system was by no means unanimous. Both the *SPD* and the unions objected strongly. In 1945, all important political groups had agreed that German capitalism had facilitated and even supported Hitler's seizure of power. Public control of concentrations of economic power was widely accepted to be the necessary antidote. As a consequence, nationalization of basic industries can even be found in the 1945 party programme of the *CDU*. But the Social Democrats and the unions went further. Both were in favour of a combination of elements of central planning with an efficiency control by the market mechanism (i.e. the law of supply and demand). The unions based their suggestions on ideas developed during the Weimar Republic. Representation in management (*Mitbestimmung* or 'co-determination') of the workers in factories and also in economic policy via 'economic councils' (*Wirtschaftsräte*) on the Federal and *Länder* level, was a cornerstone of their programme for an 'economic democracy' (*Wirtschaftsdemokratie*).

124

In the early post-war years, these and similar ideas found some support among the Western powers, especially the British with their new Labour government. But with the increasing tension between East and West, the restoration of capitalism appeared to offer a speedier and safer way of rebuilding the economy than 'experiments in socialism' (US General L. D. Clay). Although in the early post-war years the unions, as one of the least suspect organizations, supplied men for key positions in the economic administration, particularly in the British zone, they did not try to create a situation corresponding to their socialist convictions which would have been difficult to reverse afterwards. In several cases they even successfully defended existing industrial combines against Allied dismantling or de-concentration. When the Cold War and American thinking turned against union interests, earlier offers of co-determination made by employers were withdrawn. The ruling conservatives and liberals finally opted for rebuilding industry on pre-war lines.

The unions just managed to gain co-determination in the mining, iron and steel industries in 1951; and even this would hardly have been achieved without a decisive move towards a general strike. In other sectors the legislation finally passed in 1952 and 1955 respectively did not constitute a major achievement compared with the aims of the unions. But compared with other capitalist countries the results look more favourable. The 'Co-determination Act' (*Mitbestimmungsgesetz*) in 1951 (amended in 1956) gives labour 50 per cent of the votes on the 'Board of Directors' (*Aufsichtsrat*) of joint-stock companies in the industries mentioned above. (See also the article by J. Fijalkowski on the issue of co-determination for workers.) The 'Plant Organization Act' (*Betriebsverfassungsgesetz*) of 1952 gives labour the right to be represented by one-third of the members of the board of directors of joint-stock companies outside the mining, iron and steel industries. In addition, labour is represented by a 'Works Council' (*Betriebsrat*) in *all* enterprises with at least five permanent employees. The council is designed to contribute to peaceful industrial relations and to secure fair treatment of all employees. Co-determination via these councils is limited to questions such as employment and fundamental production changes as far as the latter are not an obvious consequence of a change in demand. For the Civil Service the corresponding legislation was provided by the 'Staff Representation Act' (*Personalvertretungsgesetz*) in 1955.

Apart from their demand for co-determination, the union members felt that the bitter experiences of the past indicated a need for changes in their own organization. The traditional split into socialist, liberal and Christian unions was overcome, and, under the tutelage of the Anglo-American occupation forces, sixteen mass industrial unions with a common top-level organization (*Deutscher Gewerkschaftsbund – DGB*) and one white-collar union (*Deutsche Angestelltengewerkschaft – DAG*) were formed. Together with the central agency of the employers' associations (*Bundesvereinigung Deutscher Arbeitgeberverbände – BDA*), the *DGB* and the *DAG* represent the interests of their respective members at the Federal level. The legal framework for collective bargaining was provided by the 'Collective Agreements Act' (*Tarifvertragsgesetz*) in 1949 (amended in 1952). It establishes collective agreements as legally binding on the bargaining parties and as applicable to individual contracts; their provisions constitute minimum standards, i.e. individual contracts which do not comply with certain basic requirements are null and void.

Early Years in the West: Producer-orientated Reconstruction Policy

The decision to reconstruct West Germany mainly by relying on private initiative – i.e. on market forces instead of centralized action – required strong incentives for entrepreneurial activities, especially for the formation of private capital. Tempting openings were made to enable investment to be financed out of profits. The tax burden for investors was considerably reduced:

126

(i) by scaling down personal income taxes from the confiscatory levels introduced by the Allies; (ii) by granting depreciation allowances on capital equipment which had already been written down before and during the war; and (iii) by allowing an accelerated depreciation procedure. Already in July 1948, most of the price controls and the general price freeze, in force ever since 1936, were abolished. (The most important exceptions were prices for agricultural products, basic materials like iron, coal, steel and oil, utilities and transportation, as well as rents.) This not only allowed prices to adjust to relative scarcities but also improved opportunities for self-financing of investment by price increases or holding back price cuts. Production costs had been protected by a wage freeze up to 3 November 1949. But no pressure was coming from the unions in any case. They were among those expropriated by the Nazi regime and by the currency reform, and their bargaining power was further reduced by an increase in the number of those out of work, which brought to light the disguised unemployment of the earlier years.

A dramatic surge in industrial production in the first year after the currency reform (63 per cent) was the immediate effect of the policy of favouring entrepreneurs, businessmen and debtors at the expense of people on fixed incomes, creditors, and the poor, who often were only protected against intolerable hardship by the comprehensive social insurance system. An indisputable improvement in living conditions and the relief of being freed from bureaucratic and authoritarian shackles as well as from the chaotic and humiliating conditions of a barter economy, tended to distract the public eye from privileges and subsidies which otherwise might have caused resentment.

Towards the middle of 1949 the first post-war upswing lost its momentum. The producer-orientated reconstruction policy created a growing gap between prices and consumer purchasing power. The credit squeeze, initiated at the end of 1948 in order to reduce inflationary pressures, made itself felt. The short supply of money was made more acute when converted Reichsmark bank balances stopped coming in and unexpectedly high tax revenues caused a budget surplus. Export demand reflected the down-turn of the world markets which was primarily a consequence of an American recession. On the other hand, reconstruction required a steadily growing flow of imports, and imports had just been encouraged by a first liberalization round within the European Payments Union. The resulting drop in Germany's foreign exchange reserves seemed to require an even stronger squeeze. Some opponents of the economic experiments carried out in West Germany believed that these had already failed. The discussion about which economic system would best suit the country was reopened. The *SPD* opposition, the British military government and certainly the unions favoured an aggressive full employment policy with government controls. But the West German Federal Government (and Professor Erhard in particular) held firm to the liberal concept, as did the independent Central Bank. (The Central Bank, until 1957 *Bank Deutscher Länder*, thereafter *Deutsche Bundesbank*, is an autonomous Federal institution according to Article 2 of the law concerning the *Deutsche Bundesbank*. Its functions are to regulate the note and coin circulation and the supply of credit to the economy with the aim of safeguarding the currency and to act as banker for internal as well as external payments (Article 3). The Bank is bound, as far as is consistent with its functions, to support the general economic policy of the Federal Government (Article 12). In contrast with the Bank of England it is independent of instructions of the Federal Government in the exercise of its powers (Article 12).) Both were reluctant to contemplate plans for expansion. This policy did not have to pass a final test. The outbreak of the Korean War changed the whole situation abruptly.

The Korean War: Back in the World Markets

The invasion of South Korea in 1950 gave rise to world-wide speculative and panic buying which in turn initiated a general upsurge of economic activity. In West Germany the fear of new shortages, restrictions and inflation led to a wave of hoarding of all sorts of commodities, especially raw materials. Since most of the raw materials had to be imported at soaring prices, an alarming external deficit developed within a few months. Again, demand for direct controls became pressing. But the Federal Government took a firm stand even in the face of American pressure. Policy measures were directed primarily towards credit policy. Direct controls on the economy were not introduced until the first half of 1951 and were restricted to a deliberalization of imports and a few allocation controls; exports were promoted – strictly speaking against international agreements – by tax and credit privileges.

Towards the middle of 1951 it had become quite obvious that the Korean crisis had not only produced an upsurge of imports but also a spectacular rise of exports. West Germany could offer investment goods necessary for industrial expansion in the booming Western countries. German producers had already given more attention to foreign customers because of the restrictive policies at home in the period before the Korean War and could now make full use of their newly acquired knowledge of world markets. In contrast with producers in other countries, who often had to compete for resources with a rising domestic arms production, West German export industries were able to fall back on comparatively higher capacity reserves, and small investments into war-produced bottlenecks often gave access to considerable capacity. At the same time the rebuilding of industry was successfully used for large-scale modernization. The resulting productivity increases were not eaten up by wage increases because of the unemployment which still persisted. As far as prices were concerned, the competitiveness of German exports proved to have been adequately adjusted during the international devaluation round in autumn 1949. Furthermore, the export position improved steadily after 1949 since the internal price and wage level tended to rise more slowly in West Germany than in most other European countries; hence the German mark became increasingly undervalued and the German exporters correspondingly more competitive.

One of the early instruments for checking domestic inflation was import liberalization; another was monetary restrictions which were eased only with reluctance despite the lull after the Korean crisis. As a consequence, after the middle of 1952, factory prices tended to fall slightly and the cost of living returned to the mid-1951 level. The other side of the coin was that unemployment remained comparatively high (1·38 million or 8·5 per cent in 1952). These circumstances can be considered as preconditions for West Germany's second export boom which started in 1954 (the year when her net foreign currency reserves passed the 2·5 billion dollar mark) and which consolidated the recovery after total defeat.

The unexpected, and widely discussed, West German economic revival reflects an ordering of economic objectives and a pattern of economic policy which remained basically unchanged in later years. Price stability and (indirectly) balance of payments considerations had priority over the employment situation. A socially acceptable distribution of income and wealth was ranked at the bottom of the scale, well below economic growth. Although the system of fixed exchange rates (under this system, adopted at the international conference of Bretton Woods in 1946, the value of a given currency is 'pegged' at a certain rate in relation to the American dollar and the central bank of the particular nation is required to step into the foreign exchange market as seller or buyer of the national currency whenever the market rate tends to differ, by more than a small margin, from the official exchange rate) requires, for external equilibrium, hardly more than relative price stability (i.e. keeping prices at home in line with the price trend abroad), West German economic policy consciously or unconsciously aimed at more. There were several reasons for this attitude. In the early years it was necessary to create an export surplus in order to repay foreign debts. Both the West German government and the West German public learned from the balance of payments crisis in 1950 that a country whose balance of payments shows a deficit can easily earn a bad international reputation in the system of Bretton Woods – and they learned this earlier than other countries. In addition the monetary disaster after the war, the second in the life of most Germans, had made them more sensitive towards inflationary tendencies than ever before. This, and the fact that West Germany's growth impulses came primarily from export demand, proved to be sufficient to establish export surpluses as a symbol of national virtue, irrespective of their economic and social value. This fetish and the slack labour market were considerable handicaps to the unions. Public opinion could, and still can, be turned against the unions by the accusation that their demands would endanger stability and exports.

No 'Economic Miracle' in East Germany? A Digression

The economic record of East Germany (the Soviet zone and, later, the GDR) for the first decade after the war is far less impressive than that of West Germany. To take one of the usual indicators of economic achievement, in 1950 *per capita* gross national product of the West was estimated to be only a little below the 1936 level (1950 = 92; 1936 = 100) whereas the East was almost one-third below that mark (1950 = 69). In 1957, the West German lead was still considerable (151 compared with 112). Since the economic growth of the East, from 1957 onwards, has probably not been faster than growth in the West, a gap of about 20 per cent may still exist at the end of the sixties. To attribute the early backwardness to deficiencies in the economic system which East Germany had to adopt would certainly be an over-simplification.

East Germany had to carry a much higher burden of dismantlings, reparations and occupation costs than the West. Although it possessed only a third of total German resources, the Soviet zone was forced to supply over three-quarters of all

German reparations. The East was not allowed to receive generous help within the Marshall Plan programme; it did not find a one-sided, and rather inefficient, economic integration into the Soviet bloc sufficient compensation for the cut-down of trade and communication links with the West; and it could not devote all its strength to reconstruction until the mid-fifties when Khruschev's policy of 'active co-existence' with the capitalist nations led away from exploitation to activation of East Germany's economic potential. Throughout the first decade after the war, the rebuilding of the Soviet economy had absolute priority. East Germany had to contribute to this both directly, with reparations, and by enduring a situation where, until 1951, most of her biggest industrial combines effectively belonged to a foreign power and where her foreign trade had, first of all, to fill gaps in the Soviet domestic plan requirements. The resulting economic difficulties contributed to, and were in turn aggravated by, a considerable drain on the human resources (the only asset of a country with almost no raw materials) namely the emigration of skilled workers, technicians and executives to the West.

Before examining the economic failures which can be attributed to central economic planning itself, one has to take into account the frictions which resulted from the imposition of the socialist system. This required a radical structural break, whereas the liberalization in the West only meant a return to traditional capitalist ways. The setting-up of a 'people's democracy' (*Volksdemokratie*) required a social revolution where entire groups, such as independent peasants and industrialists as well as commercial entrepreneurs, had to be dissolved. And since many members of the old middle class either chose to flee the country rather than resume their functions within the new society, or were mistrusted by the regime, a time and energy consuming attempt had to be made to prepare workers and peasants for entry into positions in the intelligentsia, bureaucracy and management.

In the economic field, 'democratic centralism' (*demokratischer*

132

Zentralismus) was introduced with a half-year economic plan (1948) and a two-year plan (1949–50). Subsequently a state planning commission after the Soviet model was created, which, in addition to short-term plans, developed so-called 'perspective plans' (*Perspektivpläne*) covering five to seven years. Private ownership of the means of production was cut back. As early as 1950 more than half of the gross national product was produced by nationalized enterprises; in 1958 their contribution had gone up to two-thirds, and in 1963 private production was reduced to a negligible 8 per cent. Not only collectivization, but also the whole rhythm of economic development, followed the Soviet pattern. Initially, priority was given, as in Russia, to the development of heavy industry, despite obvious locational disadvantages, and to the production of investment goods. Consequently, total rationing of consumer goods had to be maintained until 1952 and was not completely abolished until as late as 1958 (in West Germany rationing was practically over in 1950). The shortage of foodstuffs during the first decade reflects failures when integrating the agrarian sector into the central planning system, which remind one of similar Soviet problems. Even the politically and economically inspired planning experiments, varying between 'liberalization' (decentralization) and 'toughness' (centralization), have Soviet counterparts.

All the initial handicaps and problems mentioned above did not prevent East Germany from joining the top-ten industrial countries of the world and from becoming second in the Soviet bloc. But there is a considerable gap between industrial potential and the standard of living, although one has to take into account that, at present, the proportion of national income which in East Germany is spent on education, science and research, social security and other social goods is about two or three times as great as in West Germany. The reasons for this disparity in the standard of living between East and West Germany can be found in the unequal opportunities of the early years, in the social costs of a less thorough screening of remote parts of industry, in the general weakness of central planning systems when dealing with consumer choices, and in some costly planning errors, especially at the beginning of the sixties. But even in critical years the East German economy appears to have achieved a positive growth rate, and in good years the rate went up well above 8 per cent. There is sufficient evidence that a trend is growing towards a more consumer-orientated economy, as far as this is compatible with the general political goals of the regime.

In the seventies, East Germany's economic growth, even more than West Germany's, will largely depend on how well the problem of labour shortage can be tackled. The population balance is upset by a disproportionate number of old people as a consequence not only of the war but also of the heavy emigration to the West which could only be stopped by brute force (Berlin Wall, 1961). The working population will probably stagnate until 1975. Since participation rates are already very high and mobility of labour between Soviet bloc countries is quite low, extensive growth over the next few years is out of the question. The economic potential can, however, be further exploited by reorganization, structural change and increasing capital intensity. This possibly requires a higher rate of investment in the future. As a result, the standard of living will probably continue to lag somewhat behind that of the West. But, in any case, the economy of the German Democratic Republic seems to be definitely consolidated (disproving many Western speculations), although it is difficult to assess what price in human terms has had to be paid for this success.

Export-led Growth with Unlimited Supply of Labour: The Golden Fifties in the West.

In contrast with East Germany, West Germany was practically released from its status of occupied country as early as 1952. Allied intervention had already been reduced during the preceding years. With the Treaty of Bonn this part of Germany was to become a free state, integrated into a Western alliance.

Economically, the alliance was already firmly established in 1951 when West Germany became a founder-member of the European Coal and Steel Community which put an end to (and was politically, to some extent, a substitute for) the strict post-war controls on coal and steel production as laid down in the Ruhr statute. One condition of the Bonn treaty led to the London debts agreement of 1953 which settled West Germany's foreign liabilities resulting from the First World War debts, as well as those from immediate post-war aid (of the more than 3 billion dollars received through the Marshall Plan and other aid programmes, 1 billion had to be repaid) and restored complete responsibility for exchange control to the Federal Government. A second condition remained unfulfilled since the European Defence Community was turned down by the French Parliament. Instead, the Paris treaties of 1954 integrated West Germany into a wider NATO alliance and provided final sovereignty.

West Germany's quick and smooth integration into the Western Bloc was accompanied by a remarkable economic development. Between 1950 and 1960, her annual growth of *per capita* real gross national product averaged out at about 6·5 per cent (UK 2·2 per cent); the number of employed persons increased by some 4·4 million or about one-fifth; registered unemployment went steadily down from almost 1·6 million to 270,000 and the total capital stock was increased by about 40 per cent. Accompanied by only a moderate rise in the cost of living by an annual 1·9 per cent (UK 4·2, USA 2·1, France 5·5), private *per capita* real consumption went up by an average 6·6 per cent per annum, and the share of German commodity exports in world trade was almost doubled (to 10 per cent). The availability of labour was the most significant factor in Germany's economic growth. The increase in capital stock is estimated to come second in importance, followed by economies which mass production made possible, the special conditions of post-war recovery, and advances in technological and managerial know-how.

But how were these sources of economic growth mobilized? Many explanations have been put forward, none of which seems completely satisfactory on its own. A combination of different factors is probably more appropriate. For the critical first years, Marshall Plan aid, the national character, and 'a bit of luck', combined with a liberal economic system, seem to have played decisive roles. In order to explain the course of economic events after 1951, the elastic supply of labour, which resulted from high initial unemployment, as well as gains out of East–West migration, foreign labour markets, and reallocation from agriculture to industry, seems to be most important since it contributed much to holding down wages and maintaining high profits and investment. Both monetary policy and, at least until 1956, fiscal policy (i.e. the government's check on private economic decisions by means of taxation and public expenditures), helped to keep the price level stable. Since no aggressive full-employment policy was pursued (given the losses of production capacity caused by destruction and dismantling, the initial shortage of imports and an unemployment reserve continuously refilled by the heavy influx of refugees, it is unlikely that such a policy could have been pursued in any case), the decisive growth impulse can hardly have come from heavy consumption in the home market. And since domestic private investment – another potential impulse – is first of all derived demand (i.e. the sales prospects for the finished products at home and abroad determine the demand for capital services, i.e. investment), one has to look outside West Germany for the decisive, growth-propelling factor.

As already mentioned, given a comparatively low rate of domestic inflation and fixed exchange rates, West Germany's export-competitiveness was bound to improve. Furthermore, the comparative advantage her industry either possessed or developed, centred on goods which enjoyed a rapidly increasing demand in world-wide, post-war, industrial expansion. The benefits of this position were first realized in the Korean boom, and more of these opportunities were to come.

Looking at the first two growth cycles which West Germany experienced after 1951, a typical pattern seems to have developed. The sequence of growth impulses begins with a rapid increase in export demand, is followed by an investment push, and finishes with a wave of mass consumption. The pattern is backed up by a significant wage lag, i.e. wage increases follow increased profits at a discreet distance. This adds further impetus to investment (because profits not eroded by wage increases were ploughed back into industry in terms of new machinery, etc.) in the export sector from where the impulses spread to other parts of the economy (e.g. via increased investment). The final phase of accelerated consumption initiated by the catching-up of wages, also shows a rise in the price level. It has often been suggested, quite wrongly, that the price rise is caused primarily by rising costs (wage-price spiral). This conclusion ignores the export pull and (especially in later cycles) the lack of import competition because of inflationary tendencies abroad (with the resulting high cost of imported goods). The impact of inflation abroad was bound to become more pronounced as the nations' economies became more and more closely linked to each other and the internal supply of resources became tighter. Parallel with changes in the price-level and the increase of home demand, the balance of trade surplus (i.e. the amount by which the sale of goods and services to foreign countries exceeded the cost of goods and services bought from abroad) tended to become smaller at the end of the cycle. But, during the fifties, no trade deficit (i.e. the surplus situation in reverse) has been recorded and temporary reductions of the surplus did not disrupt the strong upward trend.

Stability and Exports: A Taboo and its Consequences

During the second growth cycle (1954-8), with an average growth rate of real national product of 7 per cent and export surpluses sometimes higher than 2 billion dollars per annum, Germany's international monetary reserves surged to more than

GERMANY TODAY

6 billion dollars at the end of 1958. This performance was achieved with quite stable prices (see Table 1). To prevent prices from rising during the final phase of the cycle, selected tariffs were reduced in 1956–7. This attempt to preserve stability by improving the competitiveness of foreign producers in German markets was combined with monetary restrictions, i.e. a slight credit squeeze. Some demand was taken out of the

Table 1   Performance of the West German Economy during past Growth Cycles

Cycle	Average rate of unemploy-ment*	Average rate of growth (a) of GNP (in 1954 prices) per cent per annum	(b) of ex-ports	Average rise of cost of living	Net foreign currency reserves† in billion $
1951–4	5·9	8·0	18·5	0·1	2·6
1954–8	3·5	7·0	13·4	2·1	6·2
1958–63	1·2	5·7	9·2	2·2	7·6
1963–7	0·8	3·7	9·6	2·7	7·6

* Registered unemployed as a percentage of the total of employed and unemployed.

† The figures refer to the end of the last year of the corresponding cycle (at the end of 1951 the reserve position was 0·4 billion dollars).

markets by a surplus of the Federal Government's revenues over its expenditures; but this budget surplus was not planned as part of anticyclical fiscal policy. Anxious that rearmament should not increase the tax burden (in 1955 taxes and social insurance contributions amounted already to some 32 per cent of Germany's gross national product, as compared with about 29 per cent in Britain), Chancellor Adenauer had initiated an advance accumulation of tax funds. The economic consequences of this operation, which had a contracting effect on the economy at the time of accumulation and an expansionary effect at the time of spending, were neglected. The tax savings were discovered by the Parliament in 1956–7 and this gave rise to a big, election-
138

inspired, spending spree. To a large extent, the spending took the form of an increase in farming subsidies and was bound to increase agricultural problems in the future. But another significant part was used to finance the early stages of a reform of the social security system.

Nothing was done to remove the excessive balance of trade surpluses although, in 1957, international currency speculation for the first time spotted the mark as an undervalued currency (i.e. people bought marks in the hope of a revaluation of the mark or in the fear of a devaluation of the pound and the French franc after which they could sell their marks at a profit). A revaluation of the mark was avoided but the balance of payments problem remained, making it increasingly difficult to control the West German price level. Several factors contributed to this development: (i) Germany had taken a lead in freeing international capital movements from controls. In 1958 the mark was declared fully convertible into other currencies. The major world currencies had become much more readily convertible than immediately after the war. Hence capital movements between countries could more easily follow international differences in exchange rates and expectations about unavoidable changes in interest rates. (ii) With the treaty founding the European Economic Community (EEC) coming into force in 1958, a new impulse was given to expand trade between the member countries. Given fixed exchange rates, this meant a further reinforcement of the links between their national price levels (through increasing and diversifying international trade). (iii) When the Common Market became effective, Germany was already a low-tariff country. This, and the step-by-step introduction of a common outer tariff for the EEC meant that the possibilities of using liberalization as an instrument to control the domestic price level were considerably reduced. (iv) In 1958-9 the German economy passed the Beveridge full employment mark (3 per cent unemployment). And with the erection of the Berlin Wall by the GDR in 1961, which stopped the inflow of skilled labour from the East, for West Germany the period of an elastic supply of labour was definitely over. A reduction in the elasticity of labour supply also meant a reduction in the elasticity of supply of domestic goods and services (i.e. the economy could more easily become overheated).

After a widespread economic downturn in the Western countries, which was led by the United States, West Germany's third business cycle (Table 1) started again with a sharp increase in export demand. This time, domestic investment received an early incentive through a number of government housing programmes, as well as interest subsidies and cheap credits for private housing projects. It was now that the factors mentioned above, affecting the control of the domestic price level, made themselves felt. When increasing shortage of labour restrained economic growth at an early stage in the cycle, which in turn meant earlier upward pressure on the price level, the Central Bank (deserted by the Federal Government which had the election in mind and pursued a pro-cyclical policy) found itself in an embarrassing situation. The mark was still undervalued since the gap between the price levels of Germany and her major trading partners (caused by her better stability record in the past) had been bridged neither by an adjustment in exchange rates (which would have made German products more expensive in terms of foreign currencies and foreign products cheaper in terms of marks), nor by a German catch-up inflation. Therefore the mark had not lost its appeal to speculators. Most other countries had just started a policy of low interest rates to encourage economic activity. Hence a rise in German interest rates to calm the economy down (by reducing the volume of credits) would have attracted foreign capital (i.e. additional supply of loanable funds) which could move easily into Germany, since currencies were freely convertible. It would therefore not have been possible to apply an effective credit squeeze. In addition, a heavy inflow of foreign capital would have increased the balance of payments surplus even further which in turn would have made the exchange rate of the mark even more suspect.

All these things happened. The *Bundesbank* first tried to push the interest rate up, with the consequences described above. Finally the Bank was forced to give its full attention to the balance of payments. With a dramatic cut of the bank rate at the height of the boom, in November 1960, the *Bundesbank* eased credit restrictions in order to prevent further capital imports and this in spite of increasing inflationary pressure.

In order to free the instruments of monetary policy to stabilize the situation, many economists suggested a change in the exchange rate of the mark. (As early as 1957 the advisory council to the Economics Ministry had suggested this strategy to remove the external disequilibrium.) But a change in the exchange rate was strongly opposed by export industries, commercial banks, farmers, by the International Monetary Fund and the administration of the Common Market, and, strangely enough, by the *Bundesbank*. To prevent a revaluation, German industry, encouraged by the Central Bank, subscribed to a billion marks development aid loan to the Federal Government. But all defensive efforts, including a discrimination against capital inflows through prohibiting interest rate payments on foreign deposits, could not prevent a heavy inflow of speculative money. Finally the mark was revalued by 4·76 per cent. This was far below what many experts considered necessary to remove the external disequilibrium. But it did provide West Germany with a stronger position in the tough negotiations over her 1961 contributions to the balance of payments costs for countries which stationed troops on German territory. At the same time it did not seriously damage the interests of the business community and could even be used as an alibi that the utmost had been done to stem inflation. These were important considerations with a general election round the corner.

But, following the cyclical pattern, the wave of price increases had been set in motion. Given the buoyancy of the markets at home and abroad, and the increasing shortage of labour, entrepreneurs had to offer wage increases which exceeded rises in productivity. And the revaluation was simply too late and too small to produce a dramatic change in the price climate. Compared with earlier years the German public had to accept a further slight increase in the rate of inflation. The fact that other countries experienced a considerably stronger erosion of their currency was cold comfort for many Germans.

Towards a Recession: The End of Non-Planning

The lull in business activity after consumption had reached its cyclical peak in the middle of 1962, only lasted about a year. Fresh impulses came from abroad during 1963 when France, Italy and the Netherlands, in particular, went through a period of considerable excess demand. With a trade surplus of about 1·2 billion dollars, unemployment down to 0·8 per cent, and nearly a million foreign workers, credit policy in 1964 again seemed to run into a dilemma. This time, the excessive trade surplus was accompanied by a heavy capital inflow, mainly because of attractive interest rates on the West German bonds market, which were not initiated by the Central Bank but reflected primarily the fact that the German capital market was still underdeveloped. The capital market had all too often been by-passed by fostering self-financing, by fixing interest rates, by granting interest subsidies and cheap direct credits, etc. (This does not mean that this policy was entirely wrong. At least as far as the housing programme was concerned it was possibly more efficient in removing the tremendous post-war shortage than the schemes adopted in other countries.)

In order to check the inflow of foreign capital it was decided, in 1964, to remove the attraction of the high interest rates by taxing away part of the interest yield accruing to foreign capital owners (*Kuponsteuer* or 'Coupon tax'). But the decisive strengthening of credit policy came from a change to credit restrictions in most Western countries. With no opposing policy trend abroad, a chance for a stabilization success seemed to be given. But then a heavy blow fell in the realm of fiscal policy.

At the beginning of 1965, an election year for the Federal

Parliament, income taxes were reduced. Although quite acceptable in social terms, since this removed some injustices, the measure was badly timed. Overall, increases in public spending (i.e. spending of Federal, *Länder* and local governments) were pushed up to twice the increase in the real national product. The Federal budget was no exception although Chancellor Erhard had previously committed himself to the principle that public spending should not increase faster than the national product. The consequence was an unplanned Federal budget deficit at a time of high pressure of private demand at home. The pro-cyclical fiscal policy added to this pressure which finally was strong enough to produce a small balance of trade deficit for the first time since 1951.

In 1966 the growth wave was running out. No new export pull was in sight and the credit squeeze became increasingly effective. Under these circumstances the financing of the Federal budget became rather difficult. The fiscal commitments contracted before the election were not restricted to the current budget alone but placed a burden on future budgets as well. And this time there seemed to be no chance that the economy would grow satisfactorily and tax revenues therefore increase and help to avoid a budget deficit. On the contrary, the economic downswing required downward revisions of revenue estimates. By postponing some fiscal 'election presents', the budget for 1966 was balanced after all. But since the downswing continued, reinforced by additional monetary restrictions, the crisis of Federal finance was merely carried over to the 1967 budget. Although the slack in demand would have justified a deficit, such an anti-cyclical policy appeared unfeasible after the fiscal escapades of 1965, not to mention institutional obstacles to any budget deficit. (At this time, orthodox commentators could still refer to Article 110 of the West German Basic Law requiring the Federal budget to be balanced annually. This stipulation was frequently interpreted as prohibiting any planned deficit although Article 115 allowed the government to obtain funds by way of credit – only via the Central

Bank – to cover expenditures for 'productive purposes'.) No support could be expected from the Central Bank which could point to the muddled state of the Federal budget, to the price level which was still rising, and to its duty to safeguard the currency. It was backed by a widespread public mistrust of deficit spending which resulted mainly from a misleading association of deficits with inflation, a combination observed during the two hyper-inflations in the past. The inability of the Federal Government to get the budget situation under control explains to a considerable extent why it finally had to resign in autumn 1966.

When the coalition of Christian Democrats and Social Democrats took over in December 1966, the economic situation had become alarming. Production and investment were rapidly declining, registered unemployment had doubled since the middle of the year, and the number of foreign workers had gone down significantly. A downward spiral of economic activity had set in. No clear signs of a change in credit policy were to be seen. The capital market was completely drained. *Länder* and local governments were desperately trying to keep pace with shrinking revenues by cutting down expenditures (leaving, for example, municipal buildings unfinished, machines idle and workers on the dole). On the Federal level, the need for an expansionary policy was increasingly recognized. But unfortunately the fiscal disorder had to be tackled as well. Given the inertia of public opinion which was still influenced by the previous fiscal failures and the resistance of the Central Bank which wanted to see a clear stabilization success, the situation of the new Government was particularly difficult.

New Men and Old Problems: The Taboo Once Again

The Federal Government, when forced to choose between giving priority to getting the budget in shape or preventing a serious recession, followed tradition and public opinion and opted for the former. This implied a budget which in its economic impact was pro-cyclical. Only late in February 1967, was it complemented by a 2·5 billion marks special investment budget in order to fight the recession. A few weeks before, a direct incentive had been given to private investment by allowing special depreciations. Following producer-orientated tradition, nothing was done to stimulate consumption. The *Bundesbank* had finally indicated a change in policy in January and was prepared to support the government in financing the special budget.

Before, and even after, the special budget was started, the *Länder* and the local governments, who decide about two-thirds of the total sum of public money spent, continued to cut down on their expenditures. This uncoordinated and, on average, still pro-cyclical fiscal policy, together with an overall sharp decline of domestic demand created by monetary restrictions (which hit hard because they were backed by a widespread restrictive trend abroad and were relaxed too late), and an only moderate export demand, produced the most serious economic set-back the West German economy has experienced since the currency reform. In the first half of 1967, real gross national product was 1·5 per cent below that of the first half of 1966, industrial production had declined to the 1965 level, and, compared with 1966, the number of employed persons went down by 800,000. At the same time, the fall in domestic demand led to a fall in imports and an additional effort to export. As a consequence the balance of trade surplus had gone up in the first half of 1967 to an all-time record of 2·1 billion dollars. Of the accepted economic goals, only price stability was really achieved.

Although the need for further fiscal action was pressing, a second emergency budget did not become effective until the autumn of 1967. Prompted by the Central Bank, many conservatives feared that further expansionary measures would threaten price stability again. Many attempts were made to talk down Germany's potential output. The mood of pessimism proved to be ill-founded since the two special budgets of the Federal Government just managed to compensate, in 1967, for the pro-cyclical cuts in the budgets of the *Länder* and the local governments.

The price paid for price stability was high, at least from a German point of view, but the fiscal escapades and the recession brought about one good thing: a definite policy change away from doctrinaire non-planning. In May 1967, the Federal Parliament passed the 'Act to Promote Stability and Growth of the Economy' (*Gesetz zur Förderung der Stabilität und des Wachstums der Wirtschaft*). A preliminary draft (orientated towards stability) had been produced by the Federal Government in July 1966. The recession and the entry of the Social Democrats into a coalition government led to the formulation of a more balanced set of economic objectives and policy instruments in the final version. Both drafts, as well as the change in economic policy under the Social Democrat Economics Minister, Professor Schiller, benefited from the public's increasing knowledge of, and willingness to discuss, economic policy. Major contributions to this discussion came from an independent Council of Economic Experts (*Sachverständigenrat zur Begutachtung der gesamtwirtschaftlichen Entwicklung*) which was set up, in 1964, to assess the economic situation. The Stability and Growth Act (i) establishes price stability, a high level of employment, external equilibrium and steady economic growth as objectives of equal rank; (ii) provides the constitutional basis for an anti-cyclical fiscal policy; (iii) requires medium-term fiscal planning on the Federal as well as on the *Länder* level; (iv) reinforces, institutionally, co-ordination between the various fiscal authorities; (v) increases the stock of policy instruments to fight cyclical and external disequilibria; and (vi) stipulates that an annual economic report, including a forecast, be drawn up by the Federal Government.

A less welcome consequence of the recession, and a challenge to the new Government, was the enormous external surplus. Although the recovery was quite strong, disproving (with growth rates for real national product of 7·2 per cent in 1968 and 8·0 per cent in 1969) all prior estimates of the short-term growth potential, the induced rise in imports did not lead to external equilibrium; the growth of exports was too strong. Again Germany experienced an export-pull as the result of her lagging price level and the reorientation of many producers to foreign markets, brought about by the previous recession at home.

In November 1968, the first heavy wave of speculation into the mark produced another of the numerous crises of the existing international monetary system. But the Federal Government refused to upvalue. Possibly in the hope of a general realignment of world currencies in the near future, a small quasi-revaluation in the area of foreign trade was introduced by a 4 per cent import subsidy and export duty on commercial trade. Although some speculative money left the country and although the Central Bank tried to push up capital exports, at the end of 1968 currency reserves were up by some 1·75 billion dollars to an all-time high of 9·3 billion dollars. In May 1969, currency markets were again upset by a growing discussion in Germany about the necessity of a revaluation in order to restore external equilibrium and in order to block the inflationary pull coming from abroad. At this time, the Federal Government was split on the issue. The Christian Democrats resisted a change in the exchange rate not only against pressure from their Social Democrat partner and the Liberal opposition party but also against the advice of the Council of Experts and other scientific advisory bodies, as well as the *Bundesbank*. Although the foreign exchange markets calmed down again, the fundamental external disequilibrium was too obvious to be removed by assurances from the Federal Chancellor that there would be no revaluation. For the first time since Bretton Woods, the exchange rate became a major issue of a country's election campaign. At the end of this campaign, in October 1969, the rate of the mark could no longer be kept pegged at the official level. After a temporary closure of the West German foreign exchange markets the rate of the mark was floated for four weeks (i.e. the *Bundesbank* no longer tried to keep the exchange rate of the mark at the previous official rate but let the rate slide

147

upwards according to the pressure of demand to find a new equilibrium level on its own). The new coalition between Social Democrats and Liberals then pegged the exchange rate again, but 8·5 per cent above the old level.

Retrospect and Prospect

Looking back at two decades of economic development, West Germany's record appears to compare not unfavourably with most of the Western industrialized countries. Growth was above average and almost uninterrupted, although not without cyclical variation. The rate of inflation was significantly below the international average but was gradually increasing. At least for the second half of the period the level of employment might be described as satisfactory, or rather more than satisfactory, with the exception of the recession in 1966–7. External equilibrium was hardly ever achieved. But this was not depressing (though it had consequences for internal stability), given the discrimination in favour of surplus countries inherent in the present international monetary system.

Was this development the outcome of an economic policy according to the blueprint of a 'social market economy'? The liberalization of the economy certainly conformed to the blueprint. And one might doubt whether more government control and central planning would have achieved such a quick post-war recovery. Defenders of the liberal doctrine can point to many forecasts produced in the early years of the Federal Republic which severely underestimated the actual speed of recovery and which would, if used as a basis for planning, have been self-fulfilling.

The requirement of a strict anti-trust legislation, however, can hardly be considered as fulfilled. The initial, tough draft of the 'Act Against Restrictive Practices' (*Gesetz gegen Wettbewerbsbeschränkungen*) was watered down under the successful attack of the business community. In the final version, passed as late as 1957, the general prohibition of cartels turned out to be a red

148

herring because of numerous exemptions. An added drawback is the position of the control authority which is weak (in contrast with the British arrangement) since it must supply proof whenever an offence is alleged.

As far as state intervention is concerned, many of the early interferences with the market mechanism could be justified on the grounds that, given the tremendous post-war shortages of essential commodities and services, either the market would have produced socially undesirable results or that private initiative alone would have been insufficient for a speedy reconstruction. But many measures designed for the advantage of the producer survived the critical initial period.

One of the most important examples of a producer-orientated bias in West German economic policy is the exchange rate policy, which facilitated export profits and later induced price waves. Repeatedly, decisions were made against consumer-interests, often in the name of an ill-defined 'international solidarity' but with the full support of the business community.

'The primacy of monetary policy' seems to have been firmly established. But this resulted less from careful policy decisions than from the independent position of the Central Bank, guaranteed by law. Often the Bank could not count on stability-orientated government action. But, as demonstrated above, the basic problem was that orthodox monetary policy, as envisaged in the 'social market economy' blueprint, can hardly perform its stabilizing functions in an integrated system of rigid exchange rates, with diverging national economic problems, priorities and policies.

In fiscal affairs, one sees a failure to put anti-cyclical measures into effect (reflecting, in part, a widespread orthodox view on budgetary policy which was sensible when the state's share in national income was negligible), lack of co-ordination between various fiscal authorities and a tendency to sacrifice the objective of stability in the period before an election.

In the field of social policy, international comparisons (e.g. of social security expenditures as a percentage of national income) show the Federal Republic in a leading position. Social policy was not only successful in alleviating, to a considerable extent, the enormous social distress left in the wake of the war (including provision for about 10 million homeless, 4 million war victims and their dependents, and millions of bombed-out people) but also, since 1955, in reforming the system of social security in a way which many observers consider exemplary. But the word 'social' probably overstates differences between the West German 'social market economy' and similar (market) economies of other capitalist countries. For a more balanced picture one has also to take into account that currency reform, producer-orientated measures as well as omissions in the field of cartel, business-cycle and exchange-rate policy left the distribution and formation of wealth to be governed by the principle 'to him that hath shall be given'. (At the end of the first decade – in 1959 – the self-employed as the major holders of wealth were estimated to have accumulated, since 1950, additional wealth per household which was at least eight times as high as in the case of blue-collar workers, almost seven times as high as for pensioners and more than twice as high as in households of white-collar workers. These ratios have to be trebled in favour of the self-employed if one adds the wealth formed in private enterprises other than corporations. See also the article by J. Fijalkowski.) Only a few half-hearted attempts to foster saving among lower income classes, and a partial denationalization of some industrial combines by introducing shares with a 'social discount', were allowed through the legislation machinery.

As to economic planning, even the most timid efforts to make the functioning of the economic system more transparent (e.g. by producing forecasts within the framework of national income accounts) were only too often interpreted as first steps towards a centrally planned, socialist economy and as a serious offence against the liberal principles of the 'social market economy'. It was not noticed that the state was interfering on a much wider scale than envisaged by the blueprint. This increased the danger that inappropriate measures might be hidden in a smoke-screen of insufficient information. And the more the economy was pushing against its capacity ceiling (in the sixties), the more pressing became the need for a finer tuning of policy measures. It was the failure to apply systematically and consistently the available policy instruments, as well as the failure to press determinedly for the necessary institutional modifications in order to achieve the major economic goals, which forced Professor Erhard (a 'man of the first hour' of the 'social market economy') to resign, and which cleared the way for the takeover by the Social Democrats.

Now the Social Democrats for the first time are leading a Federal Government (with the Liberals as junior partner). One might ask how much change in the general framework and in the emphasis placed on the various objectives of economic policy can be expected? As far as control of the business cycle is concerned, the situation has changed with the Stability and Growth Act, a greater willingness among the German public to consider changes in exchange rates and a perhaps slightly altered view of what is a tolerable rate of inflation. The (self-imposed) tasks of the new Federal Government (besides those laid down in the Stability and Growth Act) range from the pressing need to improve the social infrastructure (education in particular) to the solution of structural problems (e.g. agriculture and energy) and, linked with these, the problem of backward regions which can hardly be left any longer to the *Länder* (who are, in principle, in charge but whose performance in the past, notably in the field of education, has in general been rather poor). Most of these activities require additional funds. Part of the strategy in providing them seems to be that the government tries to keep the economy closer to its capacity limits. An upward pressure on the price level, which might result from this strategy, will be avoided, hopefully, by making use of the improved policy instruments. As complementary measures, a reinforcement of the cartel-policy is intended (by leaning towards a British-type monopolies commission), as well as a kind of incomes policy (which Minister Schiller had already started during the period of the Grand Coalition and whose first results are, like those of similar policies in other countries, hardly encouraging). The final record of the new Government does not only depend on budget restraints but also on factors like the necessity to compromise where the coalition partner takes an opposing view (as in the questions of an extension of co-determination, a tougher taxation of wealth via death duties, an improvement of the wealth formation by employees, etc.), on international arrangements (such as the Common Market regulations on agriculture), on the narrow majority of the Government in Parliament and its being in the minority, by a small margin, in the Upper House (*Bundesrat*) and last, but not least, on the skill and determination to carry out a policy programme once it has been decided upon.

Select Bibliography

H. J. ARNDT, *West Germany, Politics of Non-Planning* (New York, Syracuse, Syracuse University Press, 1966).

G. DENTON, M. FORSYTH, M. MACLENNAN, *Economic Planning and Policies in Britain, France and Germany* (London, Allen & Unwin, 1971).

H. GIERSCH, *Growth, Cycles and Exchange Rates—The Experience of West Germany*, Wiksell Lectures 1970 (Stockholm, Almquist & Wiksell, 1970).

H. LAMPERT, *Die Wirtschafts- und Sozialordnung der Bundesrepublik Deutschland* (München, Wien, Günter Olzog Verlag, 1966).

E. RICHERT, *Das Zweite Deutschland* (Frankfurt am Main, Hamburg, Fischer Verlag, 1966).

—— Sachverständigenrat zur Begutachtung der gesamtwirtschaftlichen Entwicklung, *Jahresgutachten 1964–5, 1969–70* (Stuttgart, Mainz, W. Kohlhammer, 1965, 1969).

F. STOLPER, K. HÄUSER and K. BORCHARDT, *The German Economy, 1870 to the Present* (London, Weidenfeld & Nicholson, 1967).

H. WALLICH, *Mainsprings of the German Revival* (New Haven, Yale University Press, 1955).

6 The Cultural Scene in Germany Today

W. MEYER-ERLACH

In accordance with the *Grundgesetz* of 1949 the three Western occupation zones were joined together and named: 'Federal Republic of Germany'. The title of this West German successor state of the former Reich, which expired in 1945, indicates a fundamental departure from the practice of centralism, in itself of fairly recent origin (1871) as far as the Reich was concerned. Centralism, however, had been carried to its dismal extreme during the dark period of twelve years before its total collapse at the end of the Second World War. Recklessly enforced political expediency had dictated rigid and thorough-going suppression from 'above' and this had left the cultural field almost completely barren. Relations with other nations had been severed and the wellsprings of 'undesirable' individual creativity had also been cut off. Such was the heritage left to the survivors of a cataclysm in German history whose magnitude and far-reaching effects can be compared only to the Thirty Years War when one-third of the population was killed.

For these survivors it was axiomatic that government interference be kept to an absolute minimum in order to avoid even the slightest possibility of authoritarian 'leadership'; on the other hand the few and scattered forces available for the monumental task of rebuilding the edifice of German culture were so disorganized and so weak that encouragement and some form of organization had to be provided. In order to steer between the Scylla of discredited centralization and the Charybdis of chaotic fragmentation, responsibility for cultural affairs was vested in the governments of the *Länder*.

In the examination of the way the cultural scene in Germany developed after the Second World War the effects of this dilemma will become obvious. We shall consider firstly the field of formal education and secondly other cultural phenomena.

There is no federal ministry responsible for education and the Federation has no authority to legislate on educational matters. The *Länder* are responsible for all schools. This situation is both a blessing and a curse as shall be explored in more detail below. (The details given below represent a general picture from which the conditions in a given *Land* may deviate slightly.)

Education is a basic right recognized in the constitutions of all *Länder*. Children have to attend school from the age of six for a minimum of eleven years. There are three levels of education: *Grundschulen* (primary schools), *Höhere Schulen* (secondary schools) and *Hochschulen* (post-secondary schools). Each pupil must attend a *Grundschule* for at least four years and he can stay on for another four years (five years in some *Länder* and in the German Democratic Republic) in preparation for specialized training for a particular trade or other career. A foreign language, usually English, is optional at this stage (Russian being compulsory in the GDR). Three-quarters of all students remain in this stream which is followed by three years attendance at a *Berufsschule* (vocational school) or one of the many special technical and trade schools, so that the very minimum of compulsory education, as required by law, consists of eleven years. Though all these schools offer specialized training, the general education of the pupils is not forgotten.

Instead of going on to higher grades of the *Grundschule*, students may elect to attend a secondary school after four years of elementary education. Two main streams of secondary education exist. The first is the *Mittelschule* (intermediate school). As its other name, *Realschule*, indicates, the courses offered in this stream serve the purpose of preparing the student for a wide variety of occupations in commerce, trade, administration, service activities, domestic, technical and engineering positions. *Realia* such as mathematics, natural and social sciences and at

154

least one compulsory foreign language in addition to another optional one, constitute the main body of the curriculum of this intermediate branch. The pupils spend six years at this type of school.

This leaves approximately one-sixth of the student population at the secondary school level who attend the high school proper, the *Höhere Schule*, or, as this category is generally called, the *Gymnasium*. The German usage is a good example of what E. M. Butler so aptly called 'The Tyranny of Greece over Germany'. One must look back to the era of German Classicism for the origins of this élitist establishment. The political fragmentation of Germany which began in the late Middle Ages and progressed at an ever-increasing rate led to a proliferation of semi-autonomous petty states whose courts maintained an absolutist stranglehold on the population long after the emergence of powerful nation states in England and France. For a young man of no means and humble origin the only way to improve his lot was the avenue of education. (It is interesting to speculate whether this is why the German people are considered to be *bildungshungrig*, 'thirsting for knowledge'! The German professor, with his insatiable drive for more learning, has inspired more than one humorist, starting with Voltaire and his caricature of the philosopher Leibniz in *Candide*.) Wilhelm von Humboldt (1767–1835; brother of the famous scientist and explorer, Alexander von Humboldt), the educationalist, whose influence far exceeded his brief span of office, reformed secondary and higher education with this kind of person in mind. He established what the philosopher Schelling was to call a *studium generale* which lifted German education to respectable heights – but only for an intellectual *élite*. Unfortunately this tendency for thorough education to be a prerogative of an *élite* has been handed down together with the positive elements of Humboldt's innovations and is particularly marked in the post-secondary levels of the educational system which supply the majority of professional people, including university teachers.

After the war it looked as if the *Gymnasium* was doomed and that a more pragmatic, utilitarian and realistic approach to secondary education would prevail in Germany. This is, indeed, the case in the GDR where the *Gymnasium* has been abolished completely, and by decree, as an undesirable relic of bourgeois education. In the GFR, on the contrary, the *Gymnasium* concept has actually been extended so that now three basic types exist: the first with an emphasis on classics, the second concentrating on modern languages and the third on the abstract and natural sciences. The student's level of attainment is constantly assessed throughout the school year and at the end of the year his teachers decide whether he should be transferred to a higher class or not. If his work is not judged to be satisfactory he is obliged to repeat the year. When he has completed his final year's work and passed the final exams (*Reifeprüfung* or, formerly, *Abitur*), he is eligible for admission to university.

After this necessarily brief account of the primary and secondary levels of education in Germany we turn to post-secondary education. Here the problems of the system, though perhaps no more acute, are certainly more clearly in evidence than in other sectors of education.

Soon after the end of the Second World War, a new university was put into operation, the so-called 'Free University' (*Freie Universität*) of West Berlin. Its foundation in 1948 became inevitable when the *Humboldt-Universität* in the Eastern sector was made inaccessible, to all intents and purposes, to students of the three Western sectors of Berlin. No other German university has been plagued by so many problems after what appeared to be a relatively smooth start. It became – and still is – one of the focal points of student unrest in Germany. This is only in part due to the proximity of a different social system attractive to an *élite* of bourgeois origin but with definite leftist leanings including, among others, the son of the Foreign Minister of the defunct 'Grand Coalition', Willy Brandt, now Chancellor of the GFR.

The *Freie Universität Berlin* exemplifies the many problems of the German University of the sixties and the seventies – problems whose roots reach deep down and have spread into other areas of the GFR as well. In Berlin the student Ohnesorg was killed by a bullet from the gun of a nervous police constable during the demonstrations against the state visit of the Shah of Persia in 1968. In Berlin Rudi Dutschke was hit three times by bullets from the gun of a would-be assassin for whose release he later pleaded and who finally succeeded, at the seventh attempt, in taking his own life in prison. In Berlin, rioting students smashed the almost impenetrable defences around the *Springer Haus* near the 'Berlin Wall', the headquarters of the Springer newspaper empire (investigated more closely in the chapter on the German Press in this book). It was in Berlin that restless students forced the resignation of the well-meaning but heavy-handed Lord Mayor Albertz, a minister of the church by profession. And in Berlin academic activities were paralysed at the 'Free University', leading to an exodus of well-known university teachers in protest against the successful disruption of the traditional form of higher education. At the *Freie Universität* strikes and take-overs by students have recently been matched by corresponding action by professors who felt equally badly treated. It is also in the 'Free University' that 'red cells' are functioning in departments and institutes in spite of the recent ignominious demise of the *SDS* (*Sozialistischer Deutscher Studentenbund* comparable to 'Students for a Democratic Society' in the USA) after anarchism had finally crippled the association in the year of its silver jubilee, a comparatively venerable age.

In attempting to understand how conditions in a German university have come to such a pass one must examine the historical perspective of higher education in Germany.

The 'modern' German University owes its existence to the efforts of Wilhelm von Humboldt (mentioned above) who founded the *Friedrich-Wilhelm-Universität* of Berlin (named after the ruling king and later renamed *Humboldt-Universität*) at the time of the Napoleonic domination of Prussia in 1810.

Teaching and research were the twin pillars of this institution. The concept of the equal importance of these two endeavours and of their inter-relation prevailed as the basic tenet of higher education in Germany throughout the nineteenth century. It established the reputation of the German University and has retained a firm grip on the minds of many concerned with university reform today. (James B. Conant displayed both envy and ridicule when in 1964, he termed the German University of today 'the best in the world – for the nineteenth century'.)

K. H. Becker, Prussian Minister of Education from 1919 to 1930, acknowledged the soundness of the university in principle. However, he also realized the necessity for reform in an institution which – élitistic and conservative – stayed aloof from the problems of a society undergoing profound changes in the wake of the First World War. His attempt foundered on the inertia of the institution and on the deteriorating political climate in the Weimar Republic. Although professors were officials of the state, universities enjoyed a considerable measure of autonomy within the framework of cultural federalism until 1934. Despite desperate attempts at centralization in the Third Reich (for example the nomination of Rectors by the Reich Ministry of Education) and in spite of the excessive damage done by the expulsion or flight of self-respecting scholars and by the compromising attitude of fellow travellers and mistaken idealists, there still existed in 1945 a working basis for the institutions of higher learning. After the Second World War, inertia thus proved to be a blessing – if not an entirely unmixed blessing.

Much of the blame for the troubles of the contemporary German University is traceable to the rigid continuation of the nineteenth-century tradition. The University remained as far removed from the majority of the population as ever before. The phenomenon of *Bildungshochmut* (arrogance of the educated) persisted. The German University had stood still and thus been bypassed by the dynamic developments in other countries. In the USA higher education had become mass education because of the great wealth of a nation that had become the undisputed first power in the world – if only for a limited time. In the USSR mass education included an unprecedentedly high percentage of children and adolescents; it had truly become general education where the most talented and devoted students were able to rise to the top of a broad-based education pyramid regardless of their origin or means – provided they were politically reliable. The growing isolation of Germany in the thirties and the early forties exacted an additional toll from the German University. The unique chance of 1945 to bridge, with one decisive effort, the gap which separated the German University from that of the most advanced Western countries and from fulfilling its own great promise was lost – perhaps irretrievably.

The German University was reconstituted as an *Ordinarienuniversität* (University of Full Professors). Power was vested in the *Fakultäten* (Theology, Philosophy, Law, Medicine, Science, etc.) and *Institute*, the Director of an Institute in this capacity being answerable to the *Land* rather than the University even if he held a chair. The emerging *Länder* hesitated to contest the more real than legal autonomy of the institutions of higher learning, here subsumed under the term 'University'. The *Rektoratsverfassung* (the 'Rector' being the constitutional head of the institution) prevailed. In-built inertia tided the institution as such over the difficult early post-war years. It was aided by the respect of a deprived and defrauded generation for the true authority of intellectual achievement. Disillusioned and abused, students flocked to the lecture halls enduring incredible hardship and material sacrifices and gratefully idealizing the fact that freedom of teaching and research existed again. Who is to reproach them for their lack of 'involvement' in changing the German University when the need for this change was not even recognized? In its effects and consequences, this situation is comparable to the Protestant Reformation of the sixteenth century out of which developed the sterile Protestant Orthodoxy. Humboldt's 'Reform-University' of 1810 had become a sacred cow so that the major effort after 1945 was first to restore the nineteenth-century German University rather than bring about a timely reform which would have combined the best features of the Anglo-Saxon and French systems with the viable elements of the German tradition.

It would be unfair to lay the blame for missing a unique opportunity exclusively at the door of the University. The political reorganization of what had become West Germany did little to help matters. Although in 1946 the Ministers of Culture of the various *Länder*, who held exclusive responsibility for higher education, recognized that inter-provincial co-operation and co-ordination were necessary, they were also convinced that the 'federal model' should be implemented to the very letter. The instituting of the 'Permanent Conference of the Ministers of Culture in the *Länder* of the Federal Republic of Germany' (*Ständige Konferenz der Kultusminister der Länder in der Bundesrepublik Deutschland*), whose decisions have to be unanimous, testifies to this rather naïve, Utopian belief.

Beginning in the mid-fifties the Federal Government began to assume an increasing share of the financial burden and to relieve the gross inequalities existing between economically strong and weak *Länder*. The Federation undertook to pay 50 per cent of the cost of rebuilding old universities or establishing new ones and to provide assistance to students under the 'Honnef Plan'. (*Honnefer Modell* – up to DM 340 per month is made available to deserving students: this plan was implemented in 1957; it has since been augmented by a special awards programme for outstanding students.) In 1957, co-operation was somewhat improved by the creation of the *Wissenschaftsrat* – a multiple compound noun of the kind so popular in German which defies easy translation. An adequate rendition would be 'Council of the Arts, Science, and Research'. It consists of thirty-nine members, with a majority taken from the professions and public life, one representative from each of the eleven *Länder* and a minority of only six members representing the Federation. The difficulty with this arrangement lies in

160

the fact that the council may only make recommendations, whose implementation it cannot enforce. Horror of extreme centralization had cast such a shadow that, with typical German efficiency and single-mindedness, the counter-solution overshot the mark and led to the institutionalization of 'ideal' democracy tantamount to practical inefficiency. Although the scope of its activities is far-reaching, the realization of its aims – the formulation of which has given rise to much disagreement – depends on mutual understanding, goodwill, insight and, last, but not least, financial ability. To make rapid and significant progress in this manner would constitute a superhuman achievement.

Another attempt to improve co-operation, the *Westdeutsche Rektorenkonferenz* (West German Rectors' Conference) which first met in 1949 and which has no administrative but merely an advisory function, has not met with outstanding success.

Yet another obstacle in the way of co-operation between the *Länder* has been over the extent to which they differ in terms of population, area and economic importance. They range from tiny Bremen (156 square miles and still without a university) to spacious Bavaria (27,239 square miles) and populous North Rhine Westphalia (half the size but double the population of Bavaria). Recent suggestions that the city states of Bremen and Hamburg be integrated and the territory of other *Länder* (with the exception of West Berlin) be consolidated by changing certain boundaries which would have resulted in a reduction from ten to five *Länder* of comparable size and importance have, so far, met with little enthusiasm.

As in other highly developed countries, notably England, the United States and France, the need for central financial support of cultural enterprises has increased with the need for their central co-ordination. The problem of voluntary co-operation in the GFR has been that, among others, a variety of research projects has been undertaken and recommendations have been made towards their implementation which occasionally counteract each other and are often unenforcible. Until 1962 a cumbersome mechanism for consultation and exchange of information existed in the form of Department III of the *Bundesinnenministerium* (Federal Ministry of the Interior). With the increasing financial involvement of the *Bund* in research activities, it became quite obvious that the universities, as the *loci* where teaching, education for the professions and research interact, were to be affected. Thus, in 1962, a new *Bundesministerium für Wissenschaft und Forschung* (Federal Ministry for Scientific Research) was created which determines policy and decides on federal allocations in consultation with the appropriate departments of other ministries and agencies on both federal and state levels.

It is very difficult, if not impossible, to separate the requirements of teaching and research within the jurisdiction of the German universities, and an overlapping of responsibilities is the inevitable result. Furthermore, universities and their equivalent are not the only institutions where research is carried out. There exist organizations such as the 'Max Planck Society' (Planck was awarded the Nobel Prize in Physics for developing the 'Quantum Theory') and others where research is conducted in many areas without interference from teaching duties. Then there is the area of *Grossforschung* (large scale research) conducted by industry and national or supranational agencies. The principle of the unity of research and teaching, one of the theoretical foundations of the modern German University, is, however, rapidly gaining acceptance on an international scale. In spite of its drawbacks and complications it is not likely to be abolished in the foreseeable future. Thus, the *Bund*, through its furthering of research – including financing of new buildings and entire universities and paying for the education of one-seventh of all students enrolled at institutions of higher learning under the 'Honnef Plan' (with student organizations administering the distribution of funds) – is an active and sometimes senior partner.

Greater involvement of the *Bund* than has hitherto been the case in matters pertaining to research and education, though likely to be encouraged by the Social Democrats, does not in itself provide a panacea and neither does complete centralization. Serious shortcomings still exist.

Official publications tend to stress that progress is orderly and the future of the German University secure, while playing down the obvious difficulties and the problems to be expected. It is, of course, habitual for politicians and administrators to take pride in ostensible achievements, exaggerate favourable points and minimize the significance of negative criticism. Indeed, by branding unfavourable prognoses 'sensationalism', many commentators make out that there is no cause for alarm.

However, there are very real causes for world-wide student unrest and, in addition, very specific causes for student unrest in the GFR. Why has the once so docile young German intellectual become so restive?

The age-old reference to the 'conflict of generations', although not entirely invalid, has been reduced to little more than a convenient commonplace suitable only for hiding the real issues. In fact, the concept of authoritarianism and silent obedience has been thoroughly discredited in the GFR. The appeal to authority no longer serves as a credible substitute for an inquiring and critical attitude.

Other factors have also played their part. The German *Wirtschaftswunder* (economic miracle), although eclipsed by others, especially the East German 'mini-miracle' and the Japanese 'maxi-miracle', has diverted the young away from the satisfaction of basic, material needs towards a critical examination of the 'establishment' in their prosperous society. Although it cannot always be ruled out that 'hypocrisy is the only attitude that has successfully bridged the generation gap' there is much serious striving and honest analysis behind the vocal and active attempts of academic youth to explore the anatomy of society and to re-weave the social fabric. Still, this is only part of the story.

Youth is not wholly idealistic nor impractical. On the contrary, students do get excited about very tangible matters and concrete problems. Some of these are obvious. But if it is true that in 1980 in the GFR there will be only as many university students as there are in Yugoslavia in 1970, as the national newspaper *Die Zeit* (see the chapter on the German press) predicts, then these problems are obviously complicated by the woeful discrepancy between the facilities for higher education which actually exist and those which are required.

In 1960 there were, on average, seventy-nine students to every professor. In 1938 the comparable figure had been thirty-four. The ratio has deteriorated even further since 1960. In order to improve this untenable situation, repeated suggestions have been made to reinstate the *numerus clausus*, i.e. restrict university admission which is supposedly guaranteed on obtaining the *Hochschulreife* when the student has passed the final examination at a *Gymnasium*. The number of students would be adjusted downward to the number of available places and not vice versa. In effect, this means a violation of the *Grundgesetz* wherein education has been confirmed as a basic right of the (qualified) individual. To give young people the *Hochschulreife* (which certifies, literally, that one has reached 'university maturity') and then deny them access to higher education in spite of the pressing needs of society for educated people amounts to more than indefensible casuistry: it is, in fact, tantamount to the intellectual suicide of a great *Kulturnation*, a term Germans like to apply to themselves once again. Students have clearly recognized this dilemma and are vigorously pushing for energetic, even radical, action.

The facts look grim indeed. Professors, unable to establish meaningful communication with the huge numbers of students in their lectures, often adopt an authoritarian attitude reinforced by the law of supply and demand but wholly unsuitable under changing social conditions. The shortcoming of the German University of the Weimar period, namely unwillingness to become involved with the problems of contemporary society, is thus occasionally elevated to the rank of a virtue as if history had not taught a cruel lesson. Theodor Adorno shortly before his death in 1969 refuted students who were about to put his

164

social criticism into actual effect and thereby disavowed the practicability of his suggestions, reducing his theories to the level of a meaningless mental exercise. The demise of the *Frankfurter Soziologische Schule* over its failure to reconcile theory and practice because of the stress on the former at the expense of the latter, underlined the hereditary fault of German thinkers to overcome this dichotomy by meaningful synthesis.

A number of suggestions for reform made between 1952 and 1957 seem to be esoteric from the vantage-point of the early seventies. What amazes the observer, however, is the fact that it took until 1958 at the very earliest to recognize the implications of the problem of increasing student numbers and the serious deterioration in the student–professor ratio. Even in the late sixties this problem was seen as a preponderantly quantitative one, as witnessed by the otherwise excellent and penetrating study by Gerhard Hess (*Die Deutsche Universität 1930–1970*, Godesberg, 1968). Overwhelmed by his sense of the enrolment avalanche the author favours the term *Studentenmassen* (masses of students). We assert most emphatically that it would be a grave error to review the problems of higher education in the GFR exclusively or even predominantly in terms of such 'masses'. Quantitative factors are undoubtedly involved and quantitative measures have to be taken to deal with these, but the solution must be sought via an improvement in the *quality* of higher education – and education in general – if it is to be meaningful and lasting.

The growing polarization of the academic community has resulted in confrontations not only between students and teachers but also within the teaching profession. In this process, the *Assistenten* (teaching assistants) have emerged as the most numerous, homogeneous and powerful group. They are represented by the *DAK* (*Deutsche Assistenten-Konferenz*), an *ad hoc* organization which might well become institutionalized instead of dissolving, as planned, after attaining its goals. The salient feature of this development is that the *Assistenten*, far from dividing the University into two irreconcilable factions, constitute a vitally necessary cohesive and constructive element, the importance of which in both teaching and research, has largely been overlooked in the past. With the exception of tenure (i.e. a guaranteed permanent position in their university) they have in some *Länder* (early 1970 in *Hessen*) achieved virtual equality with the *Ordinarien* (full professors) who would have been unable to carry out their duties without them. Indispensable in the operations of the University and thoroughly acquainted with their disciplines, they are none the less not much older than their students and familiar with students' problems which are often similar to their own. Vigorous and resourceful, capable of evolving and implementing new ideas, experienced enough not to fall for Utopian dreams and with a vested interest in a viable University which ensures their future, they may, indeed, provide the 'missing link' between the 'producers and consumers of education' – if this simplistic comparison with the material world be permitted.

There are other problems connected with the social structure of the student population. The tendency for the University to be the almost exclusive province of an *élite* seems to be self-perpetuating and only 6 per cent of the students come from working-class families. Most come from families with an academic background and from a city environment. The lower classes and the rural population are clearly educationally underprivileged. (See also the article by J. Fijalkowski on this issue.) It is perhaps significant that, for a transitional period, discrimination tended to be exercised in the opposite direction in the GDR with the establishment of *Arbeiter- und Bauernfakultäten* (faculties exclusively for workers and peasants and their children).

What of the position of women in the more advanced levels of the educational system? In 1964, 40 per cent of the students enrolled in *Gymnasien* were female but only 36 per cent of the matriculants. 60 per cent of the students enrolled in colleges of education were women; this reflects the majority of female teachers at the primary school level. So far, the picture does not appear to be unfavourable although the female sex is slightly under-represented at the secondary school level and its share decreases further as admission to university is approached. But the present situation where only one in four graduates is a woman is perpetuated in the universities today where the same proportion is found. Clearly, no significant changes are as yet taking place. The picture is much worse as far as the teaching staff is concerned. In the early sixties only 6 per cent of the academic personnel in the institutions of higher learning were female. Of the approximately 3000 full professors only eighteen were women! Although the equality of the sexes is incorporated in the *Grundgesetz* and, theoretically, in the legal system of the GFR, the share of women drops rapidly with increasing academic rank or status. Roughly one-half of all public school teachers but less than one-third of the teachers in *Gymnasien* are women. Although conditions have somewhat improved between 1960 and 1970 there is still a serious imbalance. 70 per cent of all women with an academic education are gainfully employed (in comparison to 89 per cent of the males), which invalidates any notion that a post-secondary education might be wasted on them. On the contrary, no self-respecting nation with cultural aspirations can, in our time, afford the luxury of discriminating against a group that has consistently made such a valuable and significant contribution to the life of society and especially to academic life.

We should not pass to the wider issues of German culture without mentioning the field of adult education. Given the situation in 1945, adult education was obviously of paramount importance. *Volkshochschulen* (the term 'people's universities' is a misnomer because these do not have the status of an institution of higher learning and cannot confer degrees) began to fill the void. Their curricula, decided on jointly by students and instructors, cover a wide range of interests but are not formalized or structured as those of regular secondary or post-secondary educational institutions. They attract considerable numbers of students by offering opportunities for broadening one's knowledge, sharpening one's critical faculties and making one more aware of society, without the coercion of a rigorous programme of studies. In the mid-sixties 1200 of these *Abendschulen* existed with nearly 5000 branches attended by 6 million people. On the whole they have proved a most successful experiment and constitute, in fact, a democratic branch of the educational system with far-reaching independence from government agencies. Although they depend on the provision of suitable buildings, usually schools, their operational funds flow from a variety of sources including unions and churches. This diversity has not hampered their growth; on the contrary it has facilitated a considerable measure of autonomy. They are organized in associations at the state and federal levels. The churches make additional efforts in providing continuing education. Eighteen *Evangelische Akademien* of the Protestant Church are affiliated with the *Landeskirchen*. (In Germany, since the time of Luther's Reformation, the Protestant Church has had a tradition of being organized according to state boundaries with an – often unfortunate – overlap of the political and the religious spheres.) The bishoprics of the Catholic Church have similar facilities. All these institutions are distinguished by their pragmatic approach to the problems of modern society, but they are hampered by the lack of recognition which excludes them from the formal system of education.

The libraries must be included in a survey of 'continuing education' at whatever level. The *Deutsche Bibliotheksverband* (Association of German Libraries) is the organization of all communal libraries which cater for 80 per cent of the entire population. In the mid-sixties 40 million books were available at public and denominational libraries. Expenditure amounted to less than DM 3 per person within the area covered by public libraries, per annum. Rural areas and inaccessible regions are increasingly served by motorized libraries but, and this is unfortunately true throughout the educational system, there are considerable differences between the numerous, well-equipped libraries in large cities or populous areas, such as the Ruhr

Valley, and their counterparts in economically backward areas like the Bavarian Forest.

We have seen that what happened in the years after 1945 cannot be held to have been a complete renewal of the fabric of German life. A case in point has been the restoration of the University to what is virtually its pre-1930 form – a retrograde step which many young people are protesting vigorously. In this essay on German culture, education has had the lion's share because education is primarily aimed at the young, who, we fervently hope, will provide the impetus necessary to attempt new solutions instead of repeating old mistakes. Any cultural effort is doomed to failure if it does not include the phoenix-like ability of youth to explore new avenues, not to be bound by obsolete precepts and undertake the giant task, as it were, of rebuilding the image of a generation without restoring the shattered remains of the past.

We have spoken of the suicidal shortsightedness in educational planning which propels the *Bildungsnotstand* (state of emergency in education) to the brink of a *Bildungskatastrophe* (catastrophe in education). Just as, in the comity of nations, no individual nation has the right to eliminate the competition of others by war (which in our time inevitably escalates to genocide), so it is impossible for any nation to escape its responsibility to other nations by 'committing suicide' and refusing to contribute its share to the common endeavour. It is understandable that the upheavals of recent history left many Germans in a state of shock and bewilderment which made it extremely difficult for them to identify with anything. The concept of collective guilt – once abused by the Nazis – was applied to the entire nation and made what is now the 'older generation' responsible for all the evil in our world. As a nation, the Germans were not permitted to forget conveniently – although the world has since realized that evil has assumed global proportions instead of becoming extinct with the Third Reich. However, individual Germans tended to repress their abominable experience, including their major or minor personal share, and develop an *ohne mich* ('count me out') attitude which became predominant in the years after 1945. They planned never to get seriously involved in anything again.

The first three years until the *Währungsreform* in 1948 were devoted to the struggle for survival. In this period the schism of Germany was institutionalized: on the one hand, the three Western zones of occupation coalesced into the GFR in 1949 and, on the other, the Soviet occupied zone was 'shoe-horned' into the GDR, also in 1949. The former became a democratic state as witnessed by its institutions; the latter an *Einparteienstaat* (single party state). Both systems, surprisingly, survived to celebrate their twentieth anniversary with pomp and circumstance – more so in the East than in the West – in 1969. In the East, cultural activity had again become a tool *ad majorem gloriam* of the state. Loyal authors praised the achievements of the socialist liberation and of a revolution, imposed from above as usually happens with German revolutions, which had achieved political and ideological unity in combination with the highest standard of living of any country behind the 'Iron Curtain'. The Western counterpart, the GFR, was treated with equal fervour by its authors – though it expressed harsh and even brutal criticism of the achievements of a *Wirtschaftswunder* that had lost much of its glamour. These attacks were justified and conducted with complete impunity.

What brought about this state of affairs? The moral bankruptcy of 1945 was equalled by the material bankruptcy – not to speak of the political one. The Germans found themselves *in extremis*. Paul Schallück speaks of 1945 as the year *der schönen Not* (of beautiful suffering). Guilt and contrition dominated the conscience of the Germans. This constituted an ideal situation for the representatives of institutionalized religion to administer the means of divine grace entrusted to them. Indeed, the churches rose to unexpected heights of renewed importance. They became a powerful and determining factor in the cultural life of what was at that time not a nation at all. Some of the educational activities discussed above were then originated by the two great denominations, the Protestant and the Catholic Church which, as a consequence of the losses of war, had attained virtual equality in contrast to the earlier situation where the Protestant North had been dominant. Congregations increased in size and services were crowded. The feelings of church-goers were by no means unambiguous. Since authoritarian government had fallen into disrepute, some virtually replaced this with a fervent embrace of the rule of the liberators so that a high-ranking clergyman had to caution his flock with the admonition: 'Even the wind blowing from on high today is not the Holy Spirit'! The material basis of the nation had been destroyed to such an extent that many lived in a state of acute want and deprivation. Food was rationed to ensure equitable distribution but there was not always enough food available to make up the meagre basic allowances. Excluded from active participation in world affairs and relegated to the status of the thief on the cross, the Germans' chances for re-spiritualization were extremely favourable in these first three years after the Second World War. The prospects for material recovery were so slim as to be practically non-existent. This lack of an outlet for productive activities diverted the interest and the energies of many towards culture. Participating actively, or as grateful audiences, the people brought about an unprecedented up-swing in all segments of the performing arts with the fine arts trailing behind because of unfavourable material conditions. Even if there were few outstanding performers, many gifted talents had survived and there was the indestructible reservoir of the world's greatest music and the world's great literature untainted by national allegiance and accessible even to the second-class humans who had been put 'off limits' (which was in fact a sign placed on German homes by the occupation forces). The secular process of a revival of baroque music dominated by Johann Sebastian Bach and his musical dynasty reached a new peak whence it has continued to inspire modern music in general. It is the synthesis between creative achieve-ment and explicit religious devotion which made this music even more important than the practising of religion in traditional forms. For although the great churches had survived the holocaust, they had not remained entirely spotless, as the passionate indictment of Hochhuth's *Der Stellvertreter* (*The Representative*) was to show later. In contrast, a performance of, for example, Bach's *Musikalisches Opfer* by the *Stuttgarter Kammerorchester* under Karl Münchinger was not merely a sacrificial offering in music (as the title indicates) but became in 1945 an act of atonement for the past. Overcoming the greatest difficulties of time and space and prevailing against incredible handicaps the cultural efforts made in Germany in these years virtually secured the spiritual survival of the downtrodden masses and prevented their radicalization – a distinct possibility which would have taken the nation almost full circle in the opposite direction.

In retrospect Ivo Frenzel asks the rhetorical question whether the philosophical beginning of the years following 1945 was anything more than *ein schönes Umsonst* ('a beautiful "in vain" '). The nostalgic undertone of this question cannot be disregarded for we now know that the spiritual upsurge of this period has had no lasting effect, though one might argue that a secularized form of spiritual revival has taken place in the GDR. (However, we must leave this last issue aside and concentrate on the GFR.)

The crucial event was the introduction of Ludwig Erhard's *Soziale Marktwirtschaft* (see the chapter by M. E. Streit in this book) on the occasion of the *Währungsreform* (currency reform) in 1948 in combination with massive aid through the Marshall Plan. Suddenly it became rewarding to work for material gain – something the Germans did with fanatic determination to exonerate themselves on this plane. German society became a consumers' society.

Cultural activities have to be seen under this aspect. Indeed, it is quite legitimate to speak of *Kulturbetrieb* (commercialization of cultural efforts). The continuously improving standard of living enabled the Germans to 'invest' in culture without jeopardizing their material progress. However expenditure was limited by the invisible and imaginary boundary line which,

172

if transgressed, would signify a less rapid growth rate of the GNP (gross national product). In 1970, 70 per cent of the gross national capital was owned by 1·7 per cent of the families. This lop-sided distribution of wealth has resulted in considerable humanitarian and cultural investments on the part of the 'over-privileged'. These, however, are insufficient to compensate for the adverse social effect of the unjustified accumulation of wealth in the hands of so few. The most glaring insufficiency is the undercapitalization of the educational sector which, if not energetically corrected, will have the gravest consequences far beyond the cultural field.

The economist, John Kenneth Galbraith, has accused the USA of insufficient public investment. Things may not be as bad in the GFR where one of the beneficial consequences of the *Kleinstaaterei* ('abundance of petty states'; more than 300 of them existed after 1648 following the Thirty Years War) in Germany was a proliferation of cultural activities – even if these were rarely first-rate as in the capitals of the great West European nation-states. However, it would be well not to lose sight of the implicit danger of commercialization which, in the final analysis, makes the profit motive the decisive yardstick for any cultural endeavour.

Germany is a classical home of opera – a genre which combines music and the dramatic interest of the stage performance. It is no accident that in nineteenth-century Germany the concept of the *Gesamtkunstwerk* had been evolved by Richard Wagner who composed his own music, wrote his own libretto and wanted to incorporate all the arts in his synthetic creation. Needless to say, the composer in him prevailed and his works have had far-reaching effects on music and the related arts today.

The material prerequisites of opera in terms of buildings, facilities and staging-costs are very great and require heavy subsidies from the *Länder*. Renowned composers head the repertoire. Wagner, Verdi, Mozart, Puccini and Richard Strauss are joined by Egk, Orff, Hindemith, Berg, Blacher and others. Operettas are extremely popular, especially those of Léhar and

Strauss. Overshadowed by opera, ballet has not regained the independence and importance it had in the period between the wars, although it is used in certain dramatic productions. For the great established theatres, a certain amount of experimentation is possible since, unlike commercial enterprises, they do not depend entirely on audience support but receive subsidies. Normally, wherever possible, new, untried and experimental operas and dramas are 'tested' on the smaller stages attached to most of the modern large houses. The theatre, too, is heavily subsidized. On the average more than one in three Germans attend one performance per annum. There are approximately 140 subsidized theatres. More than half of these are municipal houses and more than one-third privately owned and operated, the *Länder* being wholly responsible for the remainder. Subsidies total half a billion marks per year, amounting to almost DM 5 per ticket and including all types of performances. Auditoria average 250 seats. Subscriptions are very popular; they enable those responsible to offer a varied programme combining the proven, such as Shakespeare, Lessing, Schiller, Hebbel, Ibsen, Chekhov, Brecht, Frisch, Dürrenmatt and others with more modern and less well-known authors. Theatre clubs contribute to stability in attendance figures as do self-contained undertakings such as the *Volksbühne* (People's Theatre) with almost half a million members in more than one hundred local associations who are entitled to tickets costing less than DM 3. Berlin no longer commands the preeminent position it held especially between the wars, but it is still a significant theatre town where, for example, the German version of *My Fair Lady* was attended by more than a million people.

The flourishing activity on the stages of the GFR does not hide the fact that the indigenous production of first-rate plays leaves much to be desired, both quantitatively and qualitatively. A case in point is Rolf Hochhuth. His *Stellvertreter, Soldaten* (*Soldiers*) and, recently, *Guerillas* have given rise to much controversy because of their documentary character, but critics tend to reject them as dramas. Public response does not always conform to the critic's verdict and Hochhuth's plays are no exception. But one wonders whether the documentary which has also been cultivated by Peter Weiss (*Marat-Sade, Trotzki*) and Günter Grass (*Die Plebejer proben den Aufstand*. In the following translation of the title – *The Plebeians Rehearse the Uprising* – the play on the verb 'proben' which means both 'attempt' and 'rehearse' could not be reproduced) is intended to replace the more traditional 'dramatic', or even 'epic' theatre such as Tankred Dorst's *Große Schmährede an der Stadtmauer* (*The Great Tirade at the Town Wall*). It is difficult to speak of a new tradition in spite of hopeful beginnings like Wolfgang Borchert's *Draussen vor der Tür* (*Outside the Front Door*) in 1947.

If it can be said that the individual German attempted to overcome his recent past by repressing it, then German authors must certainly be credited with foiling this attempt. This applies not only to drama but also to the epic and the lyric genres. Individual authors and various loosely organized groups such as *Gruppe 47*, *Gruppe 61*, who met infrequently, tried to achieve a true *Bewältigung der Vergangenheit* (overcoming the past). In the years immediately after the war, the reading and theatre-going public, starved throughout the period of authoritarian rule, sated its appetite mainly with contemporary non-German literature, and thus failed to stimulate indigenous creativity. (Or perhaps it simply wanted to close its eyes to unpleasant truths.) Contact with the outside world was thus restored. This process was helped by a number of emigrants who, hesitantly at first, but with a tremendous display of goodwill made their way back, driven not only by nostalgic sentiments but by the sincere desire to help – like Bertolt Brecht and Thomas Mann, to quote only two well-known names.

It would only cause confusion if we attempted to list a great many authors and their works in the context of this chapter; instead we shall attempt to trace the general trend of literary development in the GFR without referring to detail. A decisive factor influencing writers on both sides of the 'Iron Curtain' – but, significantly more in the East than in the West – is the continuing division of one nation into two states. Perhaps most indicative of this situation in terms of both content and title is Christa Wolf's novel: *Der geteilte Himmel* (*The Divided Sky*, 1961; *Himmel* in German generally but particularly in this context means both 'heaven' and 'sky'). The theme has been treated in many variations and has not failed to have an impact on West German readers. However, by and large, they have come to accept the fact of a division they neither wanted nor are able to overcome. The hiatus, as we tried to show, occurred in 1948–9. Since then, what is described as the *Unbehagen an der Wohlstandsgesellschaft* (uneasiness caused by the affluent society) has grown from almost imperceptible beginnings to startling proportions. If it has ever been true that man does not live by bread alone then the literature of the GFR offers ample proof. People seem to enjoy the dubious blessings of material well-being and even luxury with hectic haste and a restlessness that can only be explained as a nagging doubt about the meaning of it all. The young, most of whom have never known deprivation, starvation, coercion and the proximity of death, nevertheless feel uneasy. They have become the conscience of the nation where their elders, for pragmatic reasons, left much to be desired. All this is reflected in their behaviour. Literature, the seismograph of social and political developments, expresses this function of youth in the GFR. The immense pride pervading the *Aufbauliteratur* (literature of revolutionary reconstruction) in the GDR is completely missing, and is, in effect, a taboo in the West.

Yet the negative aspect must not be over-rated. True, literature in the GFR has condemned the past and is extremely critical of the present. But it has attempted to perform the function of the surgeon's knife, excising the malignant growth and not satisfied with the removal of mere symptoms. This literature, leaving aside the broad fringe of attempts at senseless wordplay and the – often oversexed – *Trivialliteratur*, is not nihilistic.

176

It is beginning to assert its existence vigorously and it takes issue with all aspects of life. This could not happen if authors held out no hope for the future. In spite of the hardening of the fronts separating the West from the East and the conflicts within these power constellations which are aggravated by the population explosion, in spite of the terrifying potential of the polarized groups to destroy mankind, there is hope. Thus, German literature, German culture as a whole must no longer be seen under the chauvinistic motto: *Am deutschen Wesen wird die Welt genesen* ('The German spirit will heal the world'). History has taught the Germans the fallacy of this claim as it has always punished *hubris*. But German culture today forms a significant link, a *Bindeglied* in an area where the easing of tensions is most important. Often difficult to comprehend, it may serve to continue and strengthen the dialogue between hostile camps, indeed, make a modest, but by no means insignificant, contribution to the kind of self-knowledge that will lead to deeper understanding of other men and other nations.

Select Bibliography

H. ARNTZ, *Germany Reports*, 4th ed. (Press and Information Office of the Federal Government: Wiesbaden, Franz Steiner Verlag, 1966).

—— *Facts about Germany*, 7th ed. (Press and Information Office of the Federal Government: Wiesbaden, Franz Steiner Verlag 1968). This is an abridgement of *Germany Reports*. Also available in German: *Tatsachen über Deutschland*, 8th ed. (Presse und Informationsamt der Bundesregierung: Wiesbaden, Franz Steiner Verlag, 1967).

G. HESS, *Universities in Germany 1930–1970* (Godesberg, Inter Nationes, 1968). Also available in German: *Die deutsche Universität 1930–1970* (Godesberg, Inter Nationes, 1968).

K. A. HORST, *Anatomy and Trends of Twentieth-Century German Literature* (München, Nymphenburger Verlagshandlung, 1964).

J. H. KNOLL, *The German Educational System* (Godesberg, Inter Nationes, 1967).

H. L. and H. S. KUFNER, *Das Deutschland unserer Tage* (New York, Macmillan, 1964).

G. PRIESEMANN, *Unsere Schulen* (Frankfurt, Fischer Bücherei (757), 1966).

P. SCHALLÜCK, *Deutschland* (München, Hueber Verlag, 1969).

L. SCHMIDT and D. THELEN, *Hochschulreform* (Frankfurt, Fischer Bücherei (1011), 1969).

G. STOLTENBERG, *Hochschule, Wissenschaft, Politik* (Frankfurt, Ullstein (636), 1968).

Deutsche Kulturnachrichten, a monthly (Godesberg, Inter Nationes).

'Schule, Bildung, Wissenschaft', an extract from *Deutschland Heute*, 7th ed. (Wiesbaden, 1963).

German Research Association (Wiesbaden, Franz Steiner Verlag, 1961).

'Kulturelles Leben', an extract from *Deutschland Heute*, 8th ed. (Wiesbaden, 1968).

Meet Germany, 13th ed. (Hamburg, Atlantik-Brücke, 1969).

Index

Communist Party, *see Kommunistische Partei Deutschlands*
Currency Reform, *see Währungsreform*

Dahrendorf, Ralf, 58, 60, 71, 110
Denazification, 119
Depression, the, 35, 40, 87, 112, 114
*Deutsche Angestelltengewerkschaft
(DAG)*, 126
Deutsche Demokratische Partei,
35
Deutsche Partei (DP), 101
Deutsche Reichspartei (DRP), 101
*Deutscher Gewerkschaftsbund
(DGB)*, 72, 126
Deutscher Presserat, 71
Deutschlandpolitik, 2, 12, 23
*Deutschnationale Volkspartei
(DVP)*, 29, 42, 63
devaluation, 77, 139
Dolchstoss-Legende, 2, 34
Dorst, Tankred, 175
Dürrenmatt, Friedrich, 174
Dutschke, Rudi, 157

economic miracle, *see Wirtschaftswunder*
'educational disaster', *see Bildungskatastrophe*
elections, 138-9, 142-3
Enzensberger, Hans Magnus, 53,
64-6, 70, 80, 83
equalization of burdens, *see
Lastenausgleich*
Erhard, Ludwig, 3, 6, 7, 11, 32,
48, 57, 105, 123, 128, 143, 151,
172

European Coal and Steel Com-
munity, 135
European Defence Community
(EDC), 135
European Economic Community
(EEC), 139, 152
European Payments Union
(EPU), 128
European Recovery Programme
(ERP), 85, 86, 120, 132, 135,
136, 172
expellees, 18, 89-90, 117
'extra-parliamentary opposition',
*see Ausserparlamentarische Op-
position*

Federal Constitutional Court,
see Bundesverfassungsgericht
First World War, 35, 37, 38, 87,
88, 112, 116, 118, 135, 158
*Frankfurter Allgemeine Zeitung
(FAZ)*, 64-6, 69, 75
Frankfurter Rundschau, 64
*Freie Demokratische Partei
(FDP)*, 23, 30, 31, 42, 46, 47,
48, 49, 53, 58, 66, 71, 90, 101,
102, 106, 147, 148, 151
Frisch, Max, 174

Gaulle, Charles de, 5, 6, 8
German National People's
Party, *see Deutschnationale
Volkspartei*
German Press Council, *see
Deutscher Presserat*
Gerstenmeier, Eugen, 79
*Gesamtdeutsche Volkspartei
(GVP)*, 101
Godesberger Programm, 43, 102

180

Goebbels, Joseph, 63
Grass, Günter, 1, 71, 175
Grosse Koalition, Die (The
 Grand Coalition), 12, 31, 41,
 49, 56, 58, 59, 146, 152, 156
Grotewohl, Otto, 9
Grundgesetz, 29, 31, 33, 40, 46,
 53, 57, 64, 67, 68, 70, 76, 84,
 102, 143, 153, 164, 167
Gruppe 47, 175
Gruppe 61, 175
Günther-Kommission, 71

Hallstein Doctrine, 11, 12
Handelsorganisationen, 108
Heinemann, Gustav, 3
Heuss, Theodor, 48
Hitler, Adolf, 1, 2, 21, 38, 39, 50,
 63, 111, 112, 117, 124
Hochhuth, Rolf, 172, 174–5
Hugenberg, Alfred, 63

International Monetary Fund,
 141
Iron Curtain, 39, 176

Jaspers, Karl, 52, 57, 60
Junker, 39

Khruschev, Nikita, 5, 6, 7, 132
Kiesinger, Kurt Georg, 8, 9, 10,
 12, 24, 25, 32, 59, 77
*Kommunistische Partei Deutsch-
 lands (KPD)*, 29, 30, 32, 59,
 64, 101, 107
Königsberg, 1
Korean War, 3, 128–30, 136
Kroll, Hans, 5, 6, 7, 14, 27

*Kuratorium Unteilbares Deutsch-
 land*, 25

Länder (provinces), 41, 46–7,
 103, 104, 124, 146, 151, 153,
 154, 159, 160, 161, 166, 173,
 174
Landsmannschaften (organizations of expellees), 18
Landtage (provincial parliaments), 31
Lastenausgleich, 86, 123
Locarno, 21

Mann, Golo, 71
Mann, Thomas, 71, 175
Marshall Plan, *see* European
 Recovery Programme
Michel-Kommission, 71
Mitbestimmung, 47, 102–5, 124–6
Münchinger, Karl, 172

*Nationaldemokratische Partei
 Deutschlands (NDP)*, 18, 19,
 30, 33, 38, 41, 49, 50, 53, 79,
 101
National-Socialism, 2, 28, 29, 32,
 38, 39, 46, 50, 54, 58, 59, 63,
 85, 88, 105, 111, 112, 115, 118,
 123, 127, 169
NATO, 4, 9, 14, 17, 18, 55, 65,
 66, 84, 135
Neues Deutschland, 61
Notstandsgesetze, 10, 106
Nuclear Non-Proliferation
 Treaty, *see Atomsperrvertrag*

occupation zones, 119–20, 121,
 122, 153, 170